LIVING IN YOUR FAITH

A PRACTICAL STUDY OF THE BOOK OF
ROMANS AND FINDING PEACE WITH GOD

Wendell Van Gunst

New Harbor Press
RAPID CITY, SD

Copyright © 2021 by Wendell Van Gunst.

All rights reserved. No part of this publication may be reproduced, distributed or transmitted in any form or by any means, including photocopying, recording, or other electronic or mechanical methods, without the prior written permission of the publisher, except in the case of brief quotations embodied in critical reviews and certain other noncommercial uses permitted by copyright law. For permission requests, write to the publisher, addressed "Attention: Permissions Coordinator," at the address below.

Van Gunst/New Harbor Press
1601 Mt. Rushmore Rd., Ste 3288
Rapid City, SD 57701
www.NewHarborPress.com

Ordering Information:
Quantity sales. Special discounts are available on quantity purchases by corporations, associations, and others. For details, contact the "Special Sales Department" at the address above.

Living in Your Faith / Van Gunst. -- 1st ed.
ISBN 978-1-63357-379-6

Contents

Forewords 1
Preface to This Study of Romans 5
Introduction
    A Basic Understanding of Romans 9
Romans 1:1-17
    Essence of Romans-Living in Your Faith 15
Romans 1:18 to Romans 3:20
    We're All Guilty and Need a Savior 25
Romans 4
    It Always Was about Faith 35
Romans 5
    Finding Peace with God 41
Romans 6
    How Can a Christian Keep on Sinning? 49
Romans 7
    Living under the Law: The Old Way 55
Romans 8
    Living with the Holy Spirit: The New Way 83
Romans 9

    Struggling with Election 99

Romans 10

    Confess and Believe and You Are Saved 113

Romans 11

    The Meaning of All Israel 127

Romans 12

    How to Know the Will of God 135

Conclusion

    Where It Began 143

Forewords

This is not just another book that attempts to explain Romans. This is a work of love that has spilled over and reflects the passions of the author which becomes so very apparent as one begins to read and finds out that the content is in depth without reading like a commentary and is arresting in spirit in that it reflects the soul of the writer. Wendell has captured my mind, my interest and my soul's inner sanctum.

"Living in Your Faith" is certainly the key description of Romans. You will profit most if you open your bible, get a pen, and be prepared to underline because not only will you underline in your bible, but you will also underline many portions of this treatise of Romans. Romans is most assuredly the book that began the reformation with another man of great passion Martin Luther. It is the book that changed Martin Luther, and as you read it becomes soundly apparent that it has changed the life of the author, Wendell Van Gunst.

This book should become mandatory reading for all those studying in seminaries and in Christian colleges.

It is so well structured that it can be taught as a primary understanding of Romans. It is predictable that it will become a book used in many Christian high school classrooms.

This book is life changing. As you read it, take your time, and digest the meat and flavor of this important work, it more than likely will change your relationship with your redeemer. You will definitely experience a greater depth of "Living in Your Faith."

Charles A. Porte

I am impressed with the amount of work you did and how you focused on the overall message and practical impact of Romans rather than focusing on single verses and their theological meanings and implications.

My reading of your work and motivation seem to me to focus on producing specific results which today are not being achieved because of not enough emphasis on these main teachings of Romans.

> 1. Incredible newness of "Living in Faith" and how that should drive every one of us too much greater spreading and living out of the Gospel more joyfully, passionately, and appropriately in our daily lives.
>
> 2. That all churches should focus much more centrally on this New Freedom from the 'Death of the Law" that would create more positive celebrative worship with resulting expectations of more joyous positive and productive lives for all of us as members of these churches.
>
> 3. More emphasis on these central teachings of Romans would result in more positive cooperation by all churches rather than focusing on small theological differences which have split churches into hundreds of often contentious and counterproductive differences based on minor issues.

Dr Dennis Hoekstra

Preface to This Study of Romans

I need to share some background to this study of the book of Romans. I was on a vacation with my family in Upper Michigan. We were staying at a cabin far away from any city or any church. It was Sunday morning and along with children and grandchildren sitting in that cabin I raised a question that had been in my mind for some time. That question was about those six words in Romans 1 that I always knew by heart as "The just shall live by faith". I asked what they thought was so unique about those six words that totally changed Martin Luther. Growing up going to church every Sunday and listening to so many Reformation Sunday sermons I could not remember hearing a real answer to that question. I read about this scared, cowering monk who lived in the monastery afraid to go to sleep. Unsure on a day-to-day basis if he died would he go to heaven or to hell. Each night trying to remember if he had remembered all his sins when he confessed them in his prayers. Almost unable to function and afraid to sleep because of the nightmares he had of hell. Then came the day when the reality of

Romans 1-17 finally changed his life. I have come to believe it really was the word "Live" in the middle of those 6 words that finally grasped Martin Luther. His peers tell the story of the change it made in his life. From that scared frightened monk. Martin Luther became the vehicle God used to change the church. He was unafraid to nail his ninety-five theses on the door of the chapel at Wittenberg. He knew it would create a huge firestorm among the leaders of the Church of his day. He knew excommunication was very probable and that death for heresy was also possible, but it did not matter anymore. Martin Luther finally understood what it meant to "live in his faith" That for me is the book of Romans.

That is the change that the book of Romans offers for all those who would follow Christ. That is the change that I believe the church needs today. A body of believers focused on changing the world, set free to follow what Jesus asked us to do. To preach the gospel to all the world and to care for the hurting along the way that is the message of Romans. **That If you confess with your mouth the Lord Jesus and believe in your heart that God raised Him from the dead you will be saved Rom 10-9**. That is the simplicity of the gospel and no Pastor, no Seminary and no Church has a right to add more conditions to what Paul said was enough.

That is the message that can change you. If you have never confessed Christ as your personal Savior, I hope this book of Romans and maybe this study of Romans will lead you to let Christ become your Savior. Then and only then can you come to have what Paul and Martin Luther finally discovered "Peace with God".

THE MESSAGE OF ROMANS IS YOU HAVE BEEN SET FREE TO BEAR FRUIT FOR GOD' S KINGDOM- LETS JUST GO AND DO IT.

Wendell Van Gunst

INTRODUCTION

A Basic Understanding of Romans

It almost seems foolish for a layperson to attempt to write a study on the book of Romans. There is no shortage of books, study guides, and commentaries on this book of the Bible. As a boy, I remember listening to my grandfather and my dad discussing the weekly radio sermons by Dr. Barnhouse while grading potatoes in the old potato cellar. Dr. Barnhouse was a famous radio preacher from the Tenth Presbyterian Church in Philadelphia, Pennsylvania. He preached for over ten years just from the book of Romans.

Most of the great preachers and teachers who have written on the book of Romans agree this Book is the constitution of the Christian faith. They agree that, to truly understand the Christian faith, you must understand Paul's teachings in the book of Romans. But for many of us who sit in the pews on Sunday, reading the books that have been written make Romans far too complicated to read let alone understand. That reality is what gives me a reason to attempt writing a study about Romans. I need to be clear that I claim no special theological insight. I am not trying to refute the great preachers who have taught this book. I have learned a lot from those writings and value their teaching.

I do however think it is important to remember Paul did not write this letter of Romans to a group of academics or theologians. Rather, he wrote it to a group of relatively new Christians who we can assume had little theology background. Surely, Paul intended that those readers would understand his letter, which makes me believe he intended that we could understand it as well.

I often wonder, if Paul ever imagined we would dissect his writings as carefully as we do today. The letter of Romans contains sixteen chapters and, in my Bible, it is about thirteen pages long. Yet Dr. Barnhouse's 4-volume set on Romans has almost 1,000 pages.

I believe that Paul's reason for writing this book was much more focused than some studies would suggest.

Paul intended that this letter would define to this young church and to all who would read this letter the magnitude of what happened through the death and the resurrection of Jesus. The words of Paul in II Cor 5:17 have always been a reminder to me of what is at stake with the gospel. There Paul wrote, "If anyone is in Christ, they are a new creation the old is gone the new has come."

I believe the book of Romans is Paul's explanation of the "old that is gone" and the "new that has come." That is the heart of Paul's letter and why it is considered the constitution of the Christian faith and why it is so important for any Christ-follower to understand it. If this study could help someone understand the "new" and, because of it, find the peace that Paul wrote about in Romans 5:1 and the same peace that Martin Luther found that changed his life, then this study will have been more than worthwhile.

The church in Jerusalem we know from Acts 21 was clearly practicing all the Jewish customs required in the law in addition to this new "Way" of Christianity. Surely, that reality was a major reason Paul wrote this letter of Romans to make clear that Christianity was "The New Way" and Judaism was the "Old Way" that was now done. That goes to the point of Paul's letter, it was to ordinary Christians like most of us, so we would understand what was now the "New Way" called Christianity.

I believe lay Christians just want to know from a practical standpoint how the contents of this letter of Romans affects their daily lives. And it does. I would love to see every Christ-follower wanting to study this book. In doing so they will see how Paul's letter to the church at Rome has so much to say about how we practice our Christian faith today.

The great chapters of Romans 7 and 8 potentially offer two very contrasting views of how we live out our lives as Christ followers. If we have a choice between these two pictures, then the choice you make will dramatically affect your daily life. I realize even as I write this that many great preachers disagree with me about these two chapters and I respect that their training far exceeds mine. There are times when I wonder if academics sometimes take precedence over logic. Much of this letter follows a logical sequence as Paul develops his understanding of the old being replaced by the new, a reality we cannot ignore.

Many studies look at Paul's letters word by word, drawing conclusions he might never have anticipated. We often take a single verse and apply it to a present circumstance in a way that I believe Paul could never have imagined. I think of Romans 8:28 that we often quote to people in the hardest of circumstances: "All things will work together for good to those that love God." As if we should all be happy in the midst of the most painful experiences. While certain verses surely demand special attention, much of Romans must be understood as larger principles Paul wants to teach. Principles that cannot be contained in a single verse but are rather taught in a group of verses that need to be taken together to understand the real meaning.

Over the years, the book of Romans has challenged me in so many ways. I have read many of the books written by great preachers like Dr. Barnhouse and Dr. Martin Lloyd Jones. I have taught this as a class and, if you looked in my Bible, the book of Romans is almost unreadable with all the markings and notes in the margins and whitespaces.

I believe that the key to understanding Romans lies in understanding the very first chapter and maybe just two verses in that chapter. The verses of Romans 1:16-17 stir the heart of every Christian, and the last part of verse 17 changed Martin Luther and brought about the greatest upheaval in the church that we know as the Reformation. Verse 16 has been on the wall of my office for many years. The words from this verse say it all: "For I am not ashamed of the gospel for it is the power of God unto salvation." For me, these words reveal why Paul was so passionate about the gospel.

So, this is my attempt at creating a study of Romans for the everyday believer. I write this study knowing my limitations but also reminding myself of Ephesians 3:20: "Unto Him who is able to do far above anything I could imagine." That verse helps me believe that God could use this study to open the book of Romans for others as He has for me. Please understand I claim no special insight nor am I a studied theologian. I am just a farm boy who has grown to love this book. That is my only claim as we start this study.

With that as the background, let us begin this study of Romans and see where God might lead us. I hope it will impact your life as much as it has mine.

ROMANS 1:1-17

Essence of Romans- Living in Your Faith

You cannot help but wonder what was in Paul's mind as he sat down to draft this letter. I am sure he never imagined when he started that it would be studied and discussed for generations. Did he start writing this letter knowing all the content he would cover? Did one thought lead to another and then to another? I think that is what happened.

The first seven verses of this book contain not only Paul's description of himself as a servant of Christ, called and set apart, which surely impacted his teaching in this book, but these verses also contain several important truths that he will teach more on later. He confirms Jesus' resurrection, he says this gospel is for all the nations Jew, and Gentile, and he mentions faith as the only source of God's grace. He also makes it clear that this gospel is about God's Son, Jesus, who was promised again and again throughout Israel's history.

I think a study on the book of Romans must start by grasping the magnitude of the content of the first chapter. While this first chapter seems a simple introduction of Paul to the church in Rome, it is much more than that. The latter part of verse 17, "The just (or righteous) shall live by faith," certainly changed Martin Luther. But these six words also radically changed the church forever. They are the source of the Reformation, surely the biggest revolution in the church's history.

These six words changed Martin Luther to the point of being willing to face excommunication from the Catholic Church and potentially execution for heresy.

I believe these six words also hold the key to how we must understand the book of Romans. Why did they have such a life-changing impact on Martin Luther? For those of us that grew up in the church, I fear they have become so familiar that we never ask why they had such an impact on Martin Luther.

I think the answer is that one little word stuck in the middle of the six words: "LIVE."

What Martin Luther finally grasped was the concept of "living by faith." I think a better understanding of these verses might be to say, "live in your faith." To live "in" one's faith is to have it become part of your everyday experience and to have it guide your life. It was this concept of living by faith rather than living based on performance that finally grasped Martin Luther.

Living by performance leaves us wondering daily if we have done enough to please God. "How can I know for sure I'm okay?" is the life Martin Luther was living until the day the truth of Romans 1:17 finally penetrated his heart. Those around him must have wondered about the change that happened in his life. Living in his faith replaced living with fear. Martin's performance was replaced by Jesus' performance.

So, what does it mean to "live in your faith"? Faith, as defined by a Christ follower, is believing that if you have accepted Jesus as your personal Savior, then Jesus' death on the cross paid for your sins. They are all gone, the sin that stood between you and heaven is now gone. Fully paid for, and you are pardoned. Set free to "live" in that assurance. This truth, found in those six words, is surely what Martin Luther finally grasped and it profoundly changed him. Luther went from living day by day, wondering if he was in good standing with God, to understanding the concept that "I believe, therefore, I am saved and certain of a future in Heaven." "Living in" that truth is what changed Martin Luther from a scared, worried monk to a confident believer. It started him on a new path. Martin Luther finally found the "Peace with God" that Paul will write about in Romans 5:1. The question now is, could this study of Romans do the same for you? Can you learn to "live in your faith" that is the way to that peace that is what Paul wants for you that is why he wrote this book?

We can only wonder what all changed for Martin Luther from that day forward. We know how profoundly it changed his belief about the practices of his church. I also wonder how it affected his prayer life or his attitude in worship. I wonder how his sense of gratitude changed and perhaps most of all, his teaching about all those subjects. Surely, Martin must have said, "Amen. Now I get it!" when he came to chapter 5 and read Paul's words: "Therefore being justified by faith, I have 'Peace with God.'"

Knowing the impact verse 17 had on Martin Luther and the profound truth in this verse for all believers, I suggest that these six words also hold the key to understanding the rest of the book. I believe Paul's purpose for writing this book was to show us what it means to "live in our faith." To live our lives every day, aware of what our faith teaches about our standing with God. Paul knew firsthand what it was like living a life based on performance, and he recognized the profound change in his own life when he started living by faith. Explaining the truth of living in faith rather than by performance was Paul's motive to write this book, and that is the focus of the first eight chapters of Romans.

In chapter 1:8, I think Paul gives us an early clue that this book is about faith. He tells the church at Rome, "Your faith is noted around the world," and again in verse 12, he talks of "encouraging each other's faith." The book of Romans, at its core, is about drawing a contrast between living in our faith and living under the law. I sense this was an all-out effort by Paul to explain the real purpose of the law and to explain a new chapter in God's redemptive plan.

Another phrase used often by Paul is "a righteousness from God." We find this phrase in many places throughout Paul's letters. Paul was intent about wanting us to know that it is not our goodness, but God's goodness transferred to us that saves us. Surely the words of Hebrews 10:11-14 say it all, but verse 14 brings it home: "For by one sacrifice He has made perfect forever those who are being made holy." These words express exactly what Paul will teach throughout this book of Romans.

I believe the words of Romans 1:16 stand as the cornerstone of everything Paul believed. This verse tells us why he was so passionate about this gospel. He must have thought of this passage over and over throughout his ministry, especially through some of the darkest days of prison life. Paul was a master at saying so much in so few words and these words surely are among his very best. I like to think of the different truths that are contained in this one verse. "I am not ashamed of the Gospel for it is the power of God unto salvation." That is the gospel Paul longed to share with the Christians in Rome. And it is the gospel he shares with all of us in the book of Romans.

Let us look at some of the background and events that shaped Paul's ministry and made him the great teacher and missionary he was. I think they help us understand his passion for the ministry God asked him to do.

1. In the book of Acts, Paul stands before King Agrippa, recounting his Damascus Road conversion. In verse 14, he remembers Jesus' words from that day, "It is hard for you to kick against the goads". When I read this, I wonder if Paul had been resisting God's call for some time. And could that be why Paul's understanding of election seemed so real to him? Then in Acts 9:15, Ananias is told by Jesus to go tell Paul that Paul "is my chosen instrument to carry my name." That must have been in Paul's mind throughout his ministry.

2. Paul surely looked at the events that led to his conversion and realized that this was all God's doing. One only has to listen to Paul as he makes his defense to King Agrippa, to realize how Paul understood his faith had come about. I find his words gripping as he tells King Agrippa in Acts 26:9-11, "I wanted nothing to do with this Christianity." He continues, telling of his work to stop the spread of the gospel. I think this is the reason Paul could talk about the power of the gospel to save (change lives). When we come to chapter 9, this helps

us understand Paul's attempt to explain the reality of election or the mystery of God's choosing. Paul saw that reality in his own life because if it were not for God's intervention, Paul knew he would not be a Christian.

3. Many have taught that Paul's greatest fear was that Christianity would become just an add-on to Judaism. This concern is born out in Paul's writings. The reference to this gospel being the way of salvation for Jew and Gentile is how Paul explains that everything has changed since Christ came. One only has to go to Acts 21:20-24 and hear James' description of the church in Jerusalem to confirm how real a possibility this was to Paul. In James' own words, he says in verse 20, "You see brother, how many thousands there are among the Jews who have believed, and they are all zealous for the Law." The church of Jerusalem was teaching Christianity as an add-on to the Jewish faith. It is why Paul will say that everything has changed and that there is only one way for both Jew and Gentile to get right with God. Paul will teach that they are all God's children and they all must come to salvation by the same path, not through keeping the law but through faith. If one needs any more proof of how convinced Paul was that this gospel was for all people you need only read Ephesians 2:11-22.

4. It is almost impossible for us to understand the challenge Paul faced. The religion that Paul knew had been in effect for centuries. He is now faced with the challenge of telling the religious establishment that this

way is no longer "the" way. He had to explain to them that their centuries-old way of getting right with God through their adherence to a law full of rules and regulations was no longer viable. Paul was now saying it is not about performance but about faith. In Galatians 3:24-25, Paul teaches that the law was never intended to save us, but rather to show us the need for a Savior. Paul will go on to teach that the real Jews to God are not natural descendants of Abraham but, rather, sons and daughters of all backgrounds who have come to Him by faith. Understanding the magnitude of Paul's challenge helps us understand why God chose "a Pharisee of the Pharisees" (Phil 3:4-6), one steeped in the law to take on this challenge. It can also help us understand why Paul talks about the death of the law so often in his writings. He obviously knew how difficult this was for his Jewish friends to accept. It makes me wonder why the church today has kept it so alive.

5. Also contained in Paul's passion for the gospel must have been Paul's understanding that the Resurrection was at the heart of this Gospel. It was his Damascus encounter with Jesus that changed everything. I cannot help but remember his words from I Cor 15:17, "If Christ has not been raised, your faith is futile; you are still in your sins." Paul saw that his task was to make Jesus known to the world. Surely, his time with Jesus in the wilderness (Gal 1:17) must have been where he came to understand that this gospel is now for everyone. It is almost hard to imagine how revolutionary that was

for the Pharisee in Paul; to be told that your religion is no longer a Jewish gospel, and this law his people had been practicing for hundreds of years was no longer relevant for a Christian. As we make our way through Paul's letter, we will read, again and again, and in many ways that the law for a Christian is dead. I still believe that the church today has never accepted the death of the law in the same way Paul did. I just wonder what more he could have said than in chapter 7:4, "You my brothers have died to the law."

ROMANS 1:18 TO ROMANS 3:20

We're All Guilty and Need a Savior

Before we start, two things you should know.

First, there are some sections of Romans that I choose to study in just that—sections. I look at what a group of verses is saying rather than what a single verse within that group is saying. That is how we will approach this section of Romans. I believe it will help us with other parts of Romans as well. Taking a group of verses together can help us understand the concept Paul wants to teach better than looking at single verses within that group.

Second, I think this next section can only be understood by the conclusion Paul comes to in Romans 3:10-20 at the end of this section. There, in Romans 3:10-20, Paul writes a scathing indictment of humanity and concludes that all of us stand guilty before God. So, it seems fair to conclude that, what precedes those verses, from chapter 1:18 to chapter 3:9, is Paul laying out the evidence for his conclusion.

So, let us start at chapter 1:18. In this verse, Paul starts a section of his letter that most agree is meant to define three general categories of people. Let us look at these categories.

Romans 1:18-32, Heathens

Here, Paul describes what most would understand as a group who live apart from any semblance of worshiping the true God. Often described as heathen, worshiping all kinds of gods but refusing to worship the true God. We can assume some of these people would never have heard of the gospel as we know it. If they have heard, they choose not to believe but rather to worship other things as Paul describes. His description of the activities of this group of people we will note later.

Romans 2:1-16, Intellectuals

This group would look at the first group and say, "Surely we are not like the heathens and cannot be put in the same category as them." This group are the educated who value their intellect and will argue that the Bible is not logical, therefore some of it cannot be true. They know the arguments related to Genesis and the difficulty of understanding some of the events recorded there. They are convinced that science proves some of the Bible to be incorrect. They would argue that if it cannot be proved, we cannot accept it.

Romans 2:17 to Romans 3:20, The Jewish Nation

Here, Paul will speak directly to the Jews, those who would argue they are God's chosen people. "Surely you cannot treat us like heathens or intellectuals. We are set apart, the chosen people of God." This category believes God has given them a special revelation of Himself, a rule book on how to get to heaven. They believe they are special to God and know the way to God. They point to their long history of being favored by God and their knowledge of God's law that was given to them and only them. They believed they were the only ones with the special law that when followed, granted them favor with God.

As Paul describes these three categories of people, he is encompassing the whole of humanity. Paul's intent here is that every person on earth would fall into one of these categories. And I think what Paul means for us to understand by these categories is that all of us stand guilty before God. The point is not to find exactly where you fit in one of the three categories, but to realize that all of us are destined for eternity apart from God.

The question we need to answer is why Paul starts here. Why does he start by pointing out that we all fall short and we are all guilty? The answer I think is simple. We do not look for a cure unless we know we are sick. We do not ask for directions unless we are lost. So, Paul begins by showing us that we are all in trouble with God; that we are all lost and in need of a compass to find our way to God. Until we accept the fact that we cannot do it ourselves, we do not want or feel the need to find a different path.

So, it really does not matter how we describe the categories Paul uses. What matters is that we understand the reality of Paul's teaching in the final verses of this section. In Romans 3:10-20, Paul speaks, in no uncertain terms, that we are all guilty and lost. There is no one good enough to find acceptance with God. That is the dilemma we all face. No matter your nationality or your religious standing in the world, we all start in the same place, apart from God, with no way to bridge the gap on our own. But Paul does not leave us there. In Chapter 3:21, Paul begins to make the case for how we get right with God. He starts to lay out the path we need to follow to escape being denied heaven and a life Paul describes as "beyond our imagination" in I Cor 2:9.

But before we move on, there are some things to take note of contained in these three categories that Paul describes. I think they are worth spending some extra time considering.

The Heathens

Paul goes to some length in chapter 1:20-23 to describe that God has revealed Himself in the world around us if we choose to see Him. We should be reminded here of Psalm 19, "The heavens declare the glory of God and the world shows His handiwork."

Paul also notes that people choose to worship other things instead of God. I am reminded of missionaries who have gone to faraway places where the gospel has never been, only to find people worshiping some form of a god. Have you ever heard the phrase "man is born with a hole in his heart that only God can fill?" Solomon says it this way in Ecclesiastes 3:11, "He (God) has set eternity in the human heart." I also think of Jesus reminding the Samaritan woman that she was searching for contentment in the wrong places. These things remind us that there are many, all over the world, who are searching for inner peace. That should challenge all of us with the task of missions.

Paul also notes when talking about this category of heathens, that man without the true God is inclined to all kinds of evil practices. Reading the daily headlines or watching the daily news reminds us how true that is.

And finally, Paul touches on the issue of homosexuality which challenges all of us, including the church today. I think it is important to note that Paul specifically speaks here to the "practices" associated with homosexuality. He does not speak to the matter of "being" homosexual, but he condemns, in very strong terms, the practices associated with homosexuality. We should understand that Paul understood how sinful practices lead us away from God and that the result is being separated from God for eternity.

The Intellectuals

I think Paul would push us to understand that intellectualism can keep us from the kind of faith needed for a Christ follower. In I Cor 1:26-31, Paul says, "God has chosen the foolish things to shame the wise." Christianity is not dependent on how smart you are but is available to all those who, by faith, accept Christ as their savior. What it depends on is acknowledging our need for help, which can be hard for those who take pride in their intellect. It is often difficult for those who are highly educated, highly logical, and who hold high places to acknowledge they must come to God by the same path as those less fortunate. In verses 7-11, Paul is making it very clear we all must come by the same path. God shows no partiality.

As you read verse 13, you might wonder if Paul is teaching that it is possible to be good enough to be accepted by God. Rather, Paul is simply saying "if" you can keep the law then you would be okay. But no one can keep the law perfectly. Paul will be very clear as he concludes this section in Romans 3:20 that no one will be declared righteous by keeping the law.

The Jewish Nation

This must have been the hardest section for Paul to write. These are his people, and he says to them from here on Jews and Gentiles will be judged by the same standard. "Have you trusted Christ alone?" Paul makes clear in Romans 2:17 that the Jews have had a very privileged position. He argues that of the three categories, the Jews should have been in the best position to accept Christ. They were there from the beginning and witnessed time and time again God's faithfulness and mercy.

Paul is also critical of how the Jews have squandered their special standing with God. He describes how their pride in following the law to a fault had gotten in the way. The Jews had started thinking of themselves as having attained a standing acceptable with God based on how good they were.

The words of Romans 2:28-29 must have made the Jews cringe. Paul does not mince words as he tells them they are only Jews if they follow Christ. It is impossible for us to understand how radical that was for a Jew to hear. For Paul to tell them they are no more a Jew than a Gentile if they reject this new gospel must have been met with gasps and angry stares.

Romans Chapter 3:21

Finally, we come to the reason Paul talked about these different categories. He wants them all, all three categories, to understand that they are in need of a Savior. They are all lost. And now that Paul has made that clear, he writes this verse: "But now apart from the law the righteousness of God has been made known, to which the Law and the Prophets testify" (Romans 3:21). It is hard to imagine any two verses with more contrast in all the Bible than going from verse 20 to verse 21 of Romans chapter 3. Surely, they are the essence of the gospel message to go from guilty before God to being declared righteous by God. I believe this verse is one that every pastor needs to grasp to understand the magnitude of its content. There are few verses that carry this much theology. And it needs to be studied carefully to truly understand all the truth it contains.

For a Christ-follower, it is hard to find any verse in the Bible that has more meaning. From the condemnation of the prior verses, Paul now lays out the hope of every believer. I believe there are two common views of our hope for eternity.

There is the world's view that you "try hard" to be good enough and if you are above-average God will accept you into heaven.

2. There is the Bible's way, "to give up" and trust in Christ.

The second way is what Paul introduces to us here in these last verses of Romans chapter 3. But it is the first part of verse 21 that sets the stage for all the theology Paul will teach through chapter 8. This verse contains the heart of the gospel "a righteousness from God that has nothing to do with the law (performance)." This is the message of Romans.

Paul will teach in chapter 4 that the way to God has always been by faith. Paul knew that the Jews had come to think it was the law. For a Jew of that day, the law was the way to acceptance by God. Because of that Jewish belief, Paul will use the next five chapters to say that the only way we come to salvation is by faith. He will teach that our faith in Jesus Christ is the only way to be accepted by God. Again, and again, he will teach that the law is "dead," the old way is gone.

This is the very heart of "living in your faith" that we discussed in chapter 1. This truth is what changed Martin Luther. Imagine what Martin Luther must have thought after he came to understand that "the just shall live by faith." I wonder what it must have been like for him to read Romans 3:21 for the first time with this new understanding. The freedom he felt must have been overwhelming!

Paul goes on in verses 21-26 to make this truth even more clear. Salvation is by God's grace alone and not based on our works. Paul says there is no part of this salvation dependent on works. In verse 27, he asks, "Where, then, is boasting?" and then answers his own question with, "It is excluded." There is no room to boast because there is nothing we can point to and say, "I did that, so I am saved." Not more bible study, or prayer time, or willpower, or financial contributions. We can contribute nothing to boast about.

Paul concludes this chapter by saying that salvation by faith upholds the law. Paul is confirming his words from chapter 3:10-20 that the law condemns all of us, and only through faith will Jesus transfer His righteousness to us. Once again, it is all about faith. The law was intended to lead us to Christ because it showed us that we were sinners in need of a Savior. When that happens, the law has been "upheld, its real purpose fulfilled."

For many of us, we have been taught from childhood onwards that hard work is rewarded with success. If you work hard at school, you will get good grades. If you work really hard at your job you will be rewarded with promotions. Then the gospel comes and says it is not about how hard you work, but about giving up on your efforts and trusting Christ. No wonder it is hard for us to accept. That is the gospel Paul is teaching us and it is no wonder he must repeat some of these truths over and over.

ROMANS 4

It Always Was about Faith

Romans 4 contains Paul's teaching that faith, not works, has always been God's plan. It was always the faith of his people that put them in a right relationship with Him. Paul uses Abraham as the example. It was Abraham's faith that declared him righteous in God's eyes. Verse 3 is clear when Paul recites a passage from Genesis 15-6 saying, "Abraham believed God and it was credited to him as righteousness." Paul is making the point that it was Abraham's unswerving belief that, even in his old age, God could provide him and his wife, Sarah, a child. God not only promises a child but offspring as many as the sand on the seashore. And even though Sarah laughed at this possibility, Abraham believed, and that belief caused God to declare him righteous. By using this example of Abraham, I think Paul wanted to teach that faith was not a new concept that

God was now adding; rather, it always was a part of God's dealings with His people.

Paul's teaching goes further when he explains that this declaration of Abraham's righteousness was prior to his circumcision, which marked him as an official member of God's new family, known as the Jewish nation. Based on this fact, Paul teaches that Abraham is not only the father of the Jews, but also everyone who comes to God by faith. In Paul's day, these followers were known as Gentiles. To Jewish ears, this must have been very hard to hear. They were the chosen nation, God's special people descended from Abraham, the great father of their faith. Christ-following Gentiles had no right and no claim to be part of Abraham's family. This truth would become a central part of Paul's teaching throughout his ministry. There is no place in the Bible that speaks more clearly about this truth than in Paul's epistle to the Ephesians in chapter 2:12-22.

Chapter 4:5 was my dad's favorite verse: "However, to the one who does not work but trusts God who justifies the ungodly, their faith is credited as righteousness." After he died, I noted in his Bible that this verse was underlined. My dad knew the impact of this truth and Paul says it over and over again. It is the heart of Romans. Faith is the way to get right with God, neither the law nor how well we perform it.

Paul uses the example that if one works for a reward then that reward is not a gift. In fact, it was earned and would therefore allow one to boast. Remember chapter 3, when Paul teaches that boasting was excluded? Verse 6 takes us back to David. Paul includes this to show that even in the days before Christ came to earth, David knew this righteousness was a gift and not a reward for good behavior. "Blessed is the one whose sin the Lord will never count against them."

Verses 16-25 are Paul's explanation of the source of Abraham's righteousness. Abraham's belief in God's promise to give Sarah a child in her old age was what declared him righteous. Paul clearly states that it was Abraham's faith that allowed him to become the Father of all nations and the father of all believers, Jewish and Gentile.

Verse 20 details that Abraham never wavered in his faith that God's promise would come true. It was this unswerving faith that God acknowledged as Abraham's source of righteousness. Faith is the only way to be declared righteous. And according to Paul, because Abraham was the first to receive that righteousness, he became the father of all who come to God by the avenue of faith.

I think it is worth noting here the difference in the teachings of Paul and James. There seems to be a contrast between what Paul is saying about "faith alone" and what James teaches in chapter 2 of his book. In James 2:20-24, James writes that Abraham was declared righteous based on his act of being willing to sacrifice his son Isaac. He goes on to say in verse 24, "You see that a person is considered righteous by what they do and not by faith alone." How can two disciples have such different views?

That question brings me to Acts 21. You will read in this passage that James, as head of the church in Jerusalem, was teaching that the law was still in effect. After James hears what Paul has been teaching, he asks Paul to take a vow to show that he still believes in the law and is still living under it. It makes sense to me that, considering James's actions in Acts 21, it is likely that some of his teachings carried over into the book he wrote.

But clearly, when you go back to Genesis 15-6, it was Abraham's faith in God's promise of a son in his old age that mattered to God. And it was this belief that accounted for his blessing from God. So, Abraham became the first to be declared righteous by God, not by any work he did but by "believing" God could give him a son in his old age.

Interesting side note:

After James demands that Paul go to the temple and take a vow saying he is still living by the law, Paul agrees and starts the purification process in the temple. But before the process is completed with a final offering in the temple, Paul is arrested by the Romans. Dr. Barnhouse, who I referenced in my introduction, suggests in one of his books that God stopped Paul from going through with that ritual by having him arrested. Paul would have gone against everything he had been teaching if he had completed that purification ceremony in the temple. An interesting thought.

ROMANS 5

Finding Peace with God

"Therefore, since we have been justified by faith, we have peace with God through our Lord Jesus Christ." Whenever I read this first verse of Chapter 5, I cannot help but think of Martin Luther. One can only imagine what Martin Luther must have felt when he read these words and could say, "Yes I now have this peace." Luther talks about the nightmares he endured from the fear of condemnation because of a sin he may have committed but had not confessed. His days were consumed with wondering if he was in or out of God's grace. Was his eternity in jeopardy? There was no peace for Luther.

But this verse says something completely different. It gives a message of peace with God that, to Luther, once seemed impossible. To hear the apostle Paul say that he could have peace with God because of his faith and not his deeds must have brought the biggest sigh of relief and a huge swell of gratitude. This was truly a life-changing verse for Luther. There would be no more nightmares and no more fear of eternity apart from God.

But what should we understand about this peace? Why is this peace now possible? Dictionaries hold two possible meanings for the word peace: 1. Peace is a state of harmony; and 2. Peace is the cessation of hostilities.

Paul is describing peace as a cessation of hostilities in this first verse of chapter 5. This "end of hostilities" is what brings about peace with God. To really understand these "hostilities," we must understand a basic truth taught in the Bible about "the wages of sin."

In Romans 6:23, Paul writes that the "wages of sin is death." This is the heart of every person's problem. Sin is what separates us from God. Remember Paul's words from Romans 3:19-20? "No one will be declared righteous in God's sight by keeping the law." Paul will go on in this chapter to teach that "in Adam, we all died." We are all separated from God because of sin and it is this problem that every person needs to solve.

Paul says in chapter 5:6-11 that this problem we all have with sin is solved only through what Christ has done. These verses are such a powerful reminder of Jesus' love for us expressed in His suffering and death to purchase our salvation. Paul reminds us that it was not us asking Jesus to die for us, but rather while we were still sinners opposed to Him, Jesus "chose" to suffer and die for us. That, Paul is saying, shows how much He loved us.

What Paul has taught, and will continue to teach, through the book of Romans is that through faith, God replaces our guilt with His righteousness. So, now think back to Chapter 3:21, where Paul says, "But now a righteousness from God has been revealed." That righteousness from God has nothing to do with our performance, just our faith.

What Martin Luther came to understand is that in God's sight, our sin is gone. What God sees when he looks at us is His own righteousness, gifted to us through our faith. If I believe this gospel, never again do I need to worry about sin separating me from God. Can you imagine how that brought peace to Martin Luther?

Romans 8 will take us even deeper into this teaching and tell us that, by faith, we are adopted into God's family. A famous preacher, Dr. Falwell, Sr used to say that when you accept Christ, "you are as sure of heaven as if you were already there." That is the truth of this peace. It is real, and because of our faith, it is available. As Christ-followers, when we finally grasp what Paul is teaching here, we experience this "cessation of hostilities" and our hearts can be at peace with God.

I want to divert here for a moment, to suggest another reason why understanding this peace is so important.

When we come to chapters 7 and 8, this idea of peace with God will help us understand Paul's writing. It will help us answer the question of which Paul is Paul describing in chapter 7. Paul under the law or Paul living in faith? Paul without peace or Paul with peace? It will again be important to understand the bigger truths and concepts Paul is trying to teach in this book. To take verses as single, stand-alone thoughts, could contradict the bigger principal Paul is helping us understand.

As we keep the larger truths in mind, we will see that Paul goes to great lengths in this letter to show the difference between living by faith and living by performance. He wants us to see that "living in our faith" can bring us a peace that is not dependent on our outward circumstances, but rather it is a peace that lives inside of us. In Philippians 4:11, Paul says, "I have learned to be content whatever the circumstance." That is the peace that Paul says can be ours.

The second half of chapter 5 is Paul giving evidence to the fact that what Jesus did on the cross is greater than the consequences of Adam's sin. He also lays out that Adam's sin came before the law, which is what God gave to the Jewish people to help them stay faithful to God. These verses, I think, are his most convincing arguments.

Romans 5:12-19

Here Paul takes us back to Genesis to define five truths about sin, death, and the life that Jesus brought through his death on the cross.

1. Adam's sin affected all of us and brought the punishment of death ("wages of sin") to humanity.

2. Adam's act brought death; Christ's death brought life.

3. Paul uses the fact that everyone died because of Adam's sin, which happened before the law was given to Moses, to help make the point that the "wages of sin," or death, brought on by Adam, were not a consequence of not keeping the 10 Commandments but rather a consequence of Adam's original sin in the garden.

4. Paul also reminds us that one act of disobedience by Adam brought death to all, but one act of Christ brought the potential for eternal life to millions and millions.

5. Lastly, Paul reminds us that the death brought on by Adam was because of one sin. But the gift of "righteousness" from Jesus' can redeem not just one sin but all sins. Can I take us back again to Hebrews 10-14? "By one sacrifice He has made perfect forever those who are being made holy." Can we just accept that the "righteousness" Jesus offers is not limited; it covers all our sins, not part of them, not up to a certain time. No, it covers all of them. That is the point of this teaching from Paul that Jesus' sacrifice was sufficient to pay for all our sins.

It is a point Paul makes over and over throughout this book of Romans. He must have known we would have trouble accepting it.

Chapter 5:20-21

"The law was brought in so that the trespass might increase." This verse lays out the real purpose of the law. It was given to make humanity aware of their sins. This is a truth so often missed. God knew we could not keep the law. He did not give it as a way to achieve perfection and His favor. God gave us the law to help us see our sin and our need for a Savior. The Jews, however, turned that around and used the law as a benchmark to boast about their performance.

We can note here the story of the rich young ruler who came to Jesus in Luke 18:18-21 asking what must I do to inherit eternal life? Jesus says to him, "You know the commandments: do not commit adultery, do not murder, do not steal, do not give false testimony, honor your father and mother." In verse 21, the rich young ruler responds, "All these I have kept since I was a boy."

This was how the Jews came to see their performance of the daily requirements and ceremonies, they were keeping them all. So, if they were keeping these laws, then why did they need a savior to free them from their sin? But in verse 21, Paul speaks of the grace available from Christ and talks of it reigning in our lives. This, he says, happens when God's righteousness becomes ours, not by keeping the law, but by seeing our sin and asking Christ for His righteousness to become ours.

ROMANS 6

How Can a Christian Keep on Sinning?

Realizing that the breaks in chapters were not done by Paul, we need to see the direct connection between chapter 5 and 6. Paul ended chapter 5 by explaining that as the sins of all of us grew so did God's grace in that it was sufficient to cover all our sins.

Paul doing what he often does, he anticipates the questions he knows will be in the minds of those who read his letters. Here, he knows the readers will say—if God's grace grows bigger and bigger as our sins grow bigger, then why cannot we just keep sinning? God's grace will cover them all anyway.

Today, the question perhaps more often coming from the church might be as follows—if we teach that God no longer is counting our sins, that it is all about faith not performance, then will not people just sin because there are no consequences anyway?

Those are the questions Paul will answer in chapter 6.

His answer here in this chapter has so many ramifications, that we need to look at his response to these questions carefully.

Paul's response is basically the following: he puts it in the form of a question in verse 2. "By no means! We died to sin; how can we live in it any longer?" What Paul will teach us is that if you are indeed a Christ-follower then the Holy Spirit is living inside of you (note Romans 8 vs 9-10). Paul teaches that the Holy Spirit will change you from the inside, so you no longer desire the same things you did before you became a Christ-follower. In verses 3-4, he talks of being baptized into Christ. It would seem Paul is using baptism in the same way as being identified with Christ. He speaks here of being identified with the death of Christ; he is simply saying when Christ died, and you became a follower of Christ, His death brought about your death to sin. In the same language, he says when Christ rose from the dead, when you identify with Christ, you also have a new life to live.

Verse 5 should be a great comfort when Paul assures us that, just as Christ was resurrected, we, too, shall be resurrected one day. In verse 6, Paul reaffirms that our old self (before Christ) must be crucified (put to death) so that sin no longer will rule us. The latter part of verse 6 is so important here. Paul teaches "that we are no longer slaves to sin" and verse 7 concludes with "anyone who has died has been set free from sin."

Verses 8-11, Paul reinforces that, since Christ arose from the dead, He will never die again. He teaches that is also true for us if we have identified with Christ, then we have died to the consequences of sin.

Verses 12-14, here, it seems Paul is referring to willful disobedience to God when he says, "Don't offer yourselves to sinful practices but offer yourselves to God." In verse 14, he concludes again by saying sin cannot be your master because the Holy Spirit is now living in you and you are now under grace and not under the law.

Verse 15-23, Paul having just said you are under grace not under the law, he again knows the minds of the readers, so he anticipates their question—"Shall we sin since we are under grace and not the law?" It is hard for us to identify with the place the law played in the lives of Jewish people who for centuries lived their lives around the rules of the law. For them to hear these words from him, Paul knows is very hard for them to accept. I think it is why some of this seems so repetitious but was so necessary for Paul to make his case to his own people.

Then Paul concludes his thoughts by comparing what they gained from the former way of living (prior to becoming a Christ-follower) with the new way, saying it led to things they are now ashamed of. Then, he reminds them in verse 22 that, now, living this new life of being slaves to Christ, their reward is holiness (no longer a sinner), which gives them eternal life. It is important to note here that this holiness does not come from being good, but rather from our association (being a slave) to Christ. His righteousness is now ours.

Verse 23:

"For the wages of sin is death but the gift of God is eternal life." Here, in such few words, Paul communicates some important truths.

1. Sin is what separates us from God and brings spiritual death. It is worth noting Paul uses the singular word sin and not sins. The implication is one sin is enough to bring death. That is what we know from Genesis account of Adam And Eve; one sin brought separation from God. Remember Romans 5-16b, where Paul taught us that it was one sin that brought condemnation for all of us.

2. Then Paul will again remind us it is God's "gift" that brings eternal life. Not by being good, not because we ask God daily for forgiveness, the gift of faith and our exercising of that faith is the key to open the doors of heaven nothing else.

3. In closing this chapter with this verse, I just want to look ahead to Romans 8-2. There, Paul will say, "Through Christ you have been set free from the law of sin and death." That verse must relate to this verse 23 of chapter 6. It is this law of sin that brings death that Paul will teach is no longer in effect if you are a Christ-follower. Then and only then you are forever set free from this law of sin-brings-death.

It seems worth noting that Paul does not ever say that, once you become a Christian, you should throw away the law. The law is still a compass to help me access my walk with Christ. If I can be foolish for a moment to make a point, for instance, if I am still willfully robbing banks, then I think the law could make me see I do not have the relationship with Christ that I need. This is the essence of Paul's teaching when he says, "How shall they who have died to sin live in it any longer?" Paul is simply saying if you are living in willful disobedience, you need to ask a very hard question of yourself—"Am I really a Christ-follower?" The impact of Paul's teaching is, no, you cannot live willfully disobeying God and feel secure in your standing with God. So, the law can still play the role it was supposed to play in making me aware of my standing with Jesus.

ROMANS 7

Living under the Law: The Old Way

It is this chapter and the next chapter that I believe will bring us to the heart of why Paul wrote the book of Romans.

I want to draw your attention to a well-known verse of Paul in the book of II Corinthians that helps us understand these two chapters. In 2 Cor 5-17, Paul wrote, "Therefore, if anyone is in Christ, they are a new creation. The old is gone, the new has come." Here, Paul draws a distinction between our "old" lives, before becoming a Christ-follower, and our "new" lives, after becoming a Christ-follower. That is the essence of these two chapters of Romans. And who better to tell of this difference than Paul.

The Bible is very clear about what Paul was like before his Damascus Road "come-to-Jesus" moment. His "old" life was one of complete disbelief in who Jesus was. So much so that he led the charge to persecute and execute believers. His goal was to stamp out Christianity. But after his encounter with Jesus, while he was traveling on the road to Damascus, his life completely changed. He met Jesus and could no longer deny the truth of the gospel. In fact, not only could he not deny it, but he was compelled, at the risk of his own life, to proclaim it. In 1 Timothy 1-15, Paul describes himself as the worst of sinners. Then in verse 16 of that chapter, he says, "God chose me, the worst of sinners, to show that God's offer of forgiveness is available to any sinner."

So, who better than Paul to tell the rest of us what life is like when you are living "the old way that is gone" and then, how your life changes when you start living the "new way that has come." This is what I believe Paul is teaching when I read these two chapters. I hear Paul framing a comparison between the two ways to live, with or without Jesus. I hear him urgently describing to us the contrast of living under the old way, life as he knew it before following Christ (chapter 7) with the life he now knows, a life with Christ (chapter 8).

I understand many Biblical scholars see these chapters differently. There is much debate over who Paul is describing in verses 7-24. Is this Paul before he became a Christian or Paul after becoming a Christian? With this in our minds, let us begin our study of these two great chapters.

Chapter 7:1-6

We can only wonder why Paul felt such a strong need to teach the new Christians that the law is no longer in effect. We can only conclude what we have already noted that the law had been the way to get right with God for so many centuries. Paul knew how hard it would be to break that practice. Perhaps no place in any of Paul's letters is Paul more graphic than he is in the first 7 verses of this chapter. He clearly states that getting right with God by following the law is done. It is gone. He says in these verses that the law for a Christ-follower is dead. He does not say it is partially dead for the Christ-follower, or a little bit dead, or even almost dead. It is dead!

Paul uses the institution of marriage to make his case. He reminds his readers how marriage vows work. That the only way a marriage vow is legally broken is when the husband or wife dies. His description gets very pointed and leaves no room for misunderstanding. Paul teaches that any change in that marriage short of death, such as divorce, is not legal in God's sight. Death, Paul says, is the only legitimate way to end that relationship.

But I do not think Paul's primary intent here is really focused on the rules of marriage. It is worth noting that his words about marriage echo those of Christ in

Matthew 19. Paul is using marriage to make a very important point about the relevance of the law.

While Paul uses the example of marriage, his intent through the marriage vow's example, is to be as clear as he can about the place of the law in a Christian's life. He is making a comparison. When your marriage partner dies, you are no longer bound by that marriage agreement. When you become a Christ-follower, you die to the law. You are no longer bound by its rules and regulations.

Paul's point in this comparison was nothing short of earth-shattering for the Jewish community that he was writing to. But he leaves no room for misunderstanding. It is so important here to understand that he is writing to the Christians in Rome, both the Jews and the Gentiles, and telling them that "they have died to the law." He tells them if they have accepted Christ as their savior, the law is no longer in effect for them. In fact, it keeps them from living in their faith because it is solely based on works. And we already know what Paul has written about that. "The righteous shall live by faith." Being a Christ-follower is all about faith not performance. Let us take a more in-depth look at these verses.

Verse 4 gets at the implications of being dead to the law in our lives. What are we free to do if we are no longer under the law? What are we to do with our Christian lives if we do not have to worry about following a list of rules and regulations? What does God want from us if not to follow the law? I believe verse 4 talks directly to this. In fact, I think it stands alone in what it can teach us as Christ-followers, individually and as the church. The truth Paul teaches here should change our understanding of what God expects of a Christ-follower. If I can paraphrase Paul's words of verse 4 it would be as follows: "Now that the law is no longer in effect for you, God wants you to bear fruit for His kingdom."

Paul is saying, since Jesus paid for all your sin, you no longer need to live with worry about your standing with God. He sets you free to focus on doing His work in His kingdom. Here, we need to remember Jesus' words from John 15: "Every branch that does not bear fruit He will prune away." God is looking for fruit growers not law performers. Jesus' command to "go into all the world" is now the new law that Jesus expects of us. Paul is saying you are free to serve God, that is our challenge.

Verse 6 concludes Paul's teaching on this idea when he restates what is so clear in the prior verses. "Now by dying to what once bound us, we have been 'released' from the law so that we can serve in the new way of the Spirit and not in the old way of the written law." Surely, in any other setting "released" would not be hard for us to understand. It usually would bring a sigh of relief. But even today, I am not sure we quite get it. "Released" can mean a new focus of serving and making a difference in the world. That can be your backyard, your town or city, or it can be somewhere around the world. Paul just wants us to understand that we are free. We are released from worrying about rules and regulations to go and serve in God's kingdom. Why would we resist that or not want to accept that?

When I sit in a church service with a liturgy that includes a "confession of sin," I always think of these verses from Romans 7. It is hard for me to not to stand up and say "No! That's not what we need to hear." Didn't Paul say that is all done for a Christ-follower? Didn't Paul say you are free to serve? Didn't he say God wants you to accept that He paid it all? That forever your sins are gone. Is God still counting our sins? I do not think so. Rather, God wants to see us bearing fruit, that is what matters to Him. To suggest that we need to continue to confess sins daily surely minimizes what Christ accomplished on the cross. In Galatians 5:1, Paul says, "It is for freedom that Christ has set you free, stand firm then, do not let yourselves be burdened again by a yoke of slavery." Why would we not want to accept God's offer?

In that same church service, the "confession of sin" is usually followed by the "assurance of pardon." Here, we are often asked to recite the words of 1 John 1:9: "If we confess our sins, he is faithful and just to forgive our sins and to cleanse us from all unrighteousness." There is no doubt these words are true for a person coming into a new relationship with God, confessing that we are a sinner in need of a savior is where it all begins. But for a Christ-follower, the word "if" cannot be acceptable. It is simply inconsistent with the belief in a "righteousness that comes from God." If that confession is still required, then Martin Luther would still be having nightmares wondering if his confession was adequate. Why is it so hard for us to accept the words of Colossians 2:13?

He forgave us all our sins having cancelled the written code with its regulations that were against us and that stood opposed to us; He took it away, nailing it to the cross.

I imagine Paul sighing in frustration as he thought, "What else can I say? What else can I do to get you to understand that if you are a Christ-follower, the law is DEAD! You are free to serve and bear fruit!"

Sometimes context is key to understanding the full intent of a passage. I believe this is true for what Paul is teaching here in chapter 7. I believe there is a flow to this chapter that can help us understand who Paul is describing in the latter part of this chapter. There are four points to consider about Paul that I believe shed light on why he writes the words he writes in the order he writes them.

First, Paul begins in verses 1-7 with a strong argument that, for a Christ-follower, the law is dead. This must have been very hard for the Jewish Christians to hear. Paul was, in essence, saying that their whole system of religion, their daily rituals, and rules, were no longer valid. Surely, Paul knew the questions and disbelief that would come his way.

Secondly, in verses 7-13, Paul, being a skilled debater, anticipates those questions and makes sure he answers each one. They ask if the law was wrong or if God was mistaken when he gave the law through Moses. Paul answers this question by pointing out that the law had the important function of pointing them to Christ. The law's purpose was to be a daily reminder of their sin and their need for something outside of themselves to get rid of their sin.

In the third point in verses 14-24, Paul describes life under the law. If we look back at verse 6, Paul says: "But now by dying to what once bound us, we have been released from the law to serve in the new way of the Spirit and not in the old way of the written code." Is there any better way for Paul to illustrate "the old way" than to share from his own life as a "Pharisee of the Pharisees," what it was like to live under the law? Paul describes in detail the constant struggle to live by a set of rules, never knowing if he had done enough. These verses, I believe, are describing Paul's personal struggle living under the law.

The fourth point verse 24, "Who will rescue me from this body of death?" This was Paul's cry and it had to be Martin Luther's cry. Is there a way out of this struggle with sin? Surely, this leaves little room to doubt that these were Paul's thoughts when he was "bound to the written code," before God stopped him on that road to Damascus. These were Paul's words when he was the "old creation." On that road to Damascus, Jesus called him to a new way of living, to serve in the new way of the Spirit. Which is what Paul will passionately write about in chapter 8.

Using these four points as a guide, let us look at the remaining verses of this chapter in sequence because they are so important to the context of what Paul wants to teach. I believe they help us to better understand that there is a clear logic in this chapter.

Verse 7

This verse contains two important points worth highlighting. First, in Paul's anticipation of the question about the law being a mistake or unnecessary, it is important to note that, in the first verses of this chapter, Paul is talking about people that are already Christians. He supposes that if his readers call themselves Christians, then they were already made aware of their sin and need for Jesus. Non-Christians, however, still need the law to point them to Christ, to make them aware of their sin and inability to atone for it on their own.

Secondly, Paul takes this idea of the law being a mistake and refutes it by explaining that he would not have known that coveting was a sin except for the law. He is making it clear that this was the purpose of the law, to point out sin, and it did that for God's people for centuries. Paul assures his readers that the law was not sinful, or a mistake, or unnecessary. Rather, he teaches that his people, the Jews, distorted the law. Instead of it pointing out their sin and need for a savior, they turned it into a system of benchmarks by which they could say, "We are so good because we are keeping every law to the letter." In doing this, the law became their savior, instead of showing them their need for a Savior.

Verses 8-12

In these two verses, Paul accuses the law of causing him to sin more. He says prior to the law he did not know coveting was wrong, and once he knew the law said coveting was wrong, it made him want to covet more. It reminds me of how many of us view speed limits as guidelines not limits. When we see that the speed limit is at 55 mph, we want to go 60. When we see that the speed limit is at 70 mph, we want to go 75. This is our human sinful nature, and Paul is pointing it out in these verses. He is explaining that, before the law, he was oblivious to right and wrong with no compass. But after he knew the law, it became a compass; not to make Paul good but to let him see who he really was.

Before we leave verses 7-12, I want to look more carefully at Paul's words from verse 7 where he says, **"For I**

would not have known what coveting really was if the law had not said 'Do not covet.'"

This verse raises a very important question. Before the law was given, did people know what was sin and what was not sin? Paul says in these verses that we would not know what sin was without the law. That was the point of the law, right? To show us our sin. Let us look at some verses from other places in Romans that can only be understood in the context of what Paul is writing here in Romans 7:7. They might also be able to help us better understand the rest of chapter 7, which has brought disagreement among the best preachers and theologians. Please note that I am not quoting these texts in their entirety, but rather using the parts of these verses that relate to our study.

Romans 5:1 - "...just as sin entered through one man..."

Romans 3:25b - "In his forbearance, God had left the sins committed beforehand unpunished."

Romans 4:15 - "...because law brings wrath and where there is no law there is no transgression."

Romans 5:13 - "...for before the law was given, sin was in the world, but sin is not taken into account when there is no law."

Romans 5:20 - "The law was added so the trespass might increase."

Romans 6:7 - "Because anyone who has died has been freed from sin."

Romans 6:8 - "Now if we died with Christ..."

Romans 6:11 - "In the same way count yourselves dead to 'sin' but alive to God in Christ Jesus."

Romans 6:14 - "For sin shall not be your master because you are not under law."

Romans 6:18 - "...you have been set free from sin and have become slaves to righteousness."

Romans 6:22 - "But now you have been set free from sin."

Romans 6:23 - "For the wages of sin is death but the "gift" of God is eternal life."

Romans 7-1 - "The law has authority over a man only as long as he lives."

Romans 7:6 - "...but now by dying to what once bound us, we have been released from the law so that we serve in the new way of the Spirit and not in the old way of the written code."

Romans 7:7 - "...indeed I would not have known what sin was except through the law for I would not have known what coveting really was if the law had not said 'do not covet.'

Romans 7:7-8b - "...for apart from law sin is dead."

Romans 7:13 - "...but in order that sin might be recognized as sin."

Romans 7:18 - "I know that nothing good lives in me, that is, in my 'sinful' nature."

I would like to suggest that in these verses, Paul is teaching a concept we seldom consider in our discussion of sin and the law. In Romans 5:12, Paul reminds us that sin was a new concept and only became a reality when Adam disobeyed God in the Garden. Sin was then known as disobeying a direct command of God, "Do not eat of this tree," which Adam and Eve did. It is implied that, up to that point, Adam and Eve were without sin. But what does "without sin" mean? How would that be evident in one's life?

In Matthew 22, Jesus was asked to pick the greatest of the ten commandments. But what Jesus did was explain the essence of the entire law. His answer was simple: "Love God with all your heart, soul and mind. This is the greatest commandment. But a very close second is loving your neighbor as yourself" (Matthew 22:37-40, my paraphrase.). According to Jesus, if these two commandments are the essence of the whole law, then we can conclude that Adam and Eve were living within those two commandments prior to their eating of the fruit. This was a time of Adam and Eve before sin entered the world, a world no one has experienced since.

Now we think of Paul in verse 7 talking about how he did not know that coveting was wrong until he knew the law. That should make us wonder, after eating the fruit from the Tree of Life, what else did Adam and Eve discover was sinful for them to do? Consider the following examples from this time prior to when God gave the Law to Moses and the Israelites:

Noah despite his drunkenness is blessed by God (Gen 9-21).

Abraham lies about his wife, and God punishes Pharaoh but seems to reward Abraham (Gen 12-13).

Sarah lies about having laughed but there is no punishment (Gen 18-15).

For a second time, Abraham lies about his wife to Abimelech with no punishment (Gen 20-2).

Moses kills an Egyptian and flees for his life from Pharaoh but not from God (Exodus 2-12).

Jacob lies to his father and gets the blessing instead of Esau without punishment (Gen 27-19).

Joseph's brothers sell him and seem to go on with their lives without consequence (Gen 37-3).

The question we can ask—did Noah, Abraham, Sarah, Moses, Jacob, or Joseph's brothers know these acts were sin? It seems reasonable to believe that they didn't know, since they had not received any commandment like what Adam and Eve had. When you read the prior verses we listed, Romans 3:25b, Romans 4:15 and Romans 5:13, you sense Paul was saying that before the law, sin was not counted and therefore not punished. Yet God clearly punished some sin, for example, destroying Sodom and Gomorrah because of their sin. God also made clear to Cain that killing Abel was wrong, and he severely punished him (Gen 4-13).

Yet it seems that God did not punish the sin of those who were part of the covenant relationship He had established. That can have some importance as we consider how God deals with those who are adopted into His family. Then, when Paul writes that "you have died to the law," it takes on a new understanding of living in God's family.

It is evident God knew that, after Adam and Eve sinned, He would need to define for His followers, and really, for all humanity, some guidelines for living with a sinful nature. In Romans 5:20, Paul writes, "The law was added so the trespass might increase." Paul is getting at the heart of this issue. He is saying that the law was given so man would know what sin was. People cannot blame ignorance anymore for their wrongdoing. God laid out His guidelines that we know as the Ten Commandments so everyone would know what was wrong to God. He gave this law to point out our sin. This then becomes the purpose of the Ten Commandments given to Moses. He wanted to be very clear for his people about what was sin and the consequences.

Next came a set of complicated practices of offering sacrifices and different rituals that would help the people atone for the sins they now knew they were committing. But even this remedy became complicated. One has only to read the book of Leviticus to get an idea of the vast scope of rules and regulations the Israelites were expected to follow.

Malachi 1 is a great example of God's anger over the improper use of these regulations and rituals, especially when it came to the sacrifices required to atone for their sins. God was very clear about the requirements of an acceptable sacrifice. It had to be a perfect lamb, the best of the flock. But the people were bringing the sick, less valuable animals, and God was very clear He would not accept them.

But imagine for a moment that you are a shepherd with an exceptional flock of sheep. Your neighbor comes over, looks at your sheep, and offers you $10,000 for one of them. In your mind, you might be trying hard NOT to remember God saying that your sacrifice needs to be your best one. Your neighbor is willing to pay a lot of money for that sheep. Will God care if you bring a different sheep not as valuable but that looks just as good for a sacrifice? This is the dilemma of the law. Can you imagine the temptation to rationalize which sheep should be sacrificed to God? It could be easy to say that, just because my neighbor wants to pay that much for a sheep, does not mean it is the best one.

Then we go to Matthew 5 where Jesus expands the Ten Commandments, saying if you are angry with a brother, you have committed murder. If you look at a woman with lust, you have committed adultery. These, surely, remind us that the Ten Commandments embody requirements far beyond the Ten Commandments as written in Exodus 20.

Growing up in a church where the law was prominent, I remember the rules: You cannot skate on the pond on Sunday; you cannot play ball on Sunday; my mom prepared all the Sunday food on Saturday night to keep the Sabbath holy; there were certain card games you could not play; dancing was out; and the list could go on. What words violate taking God's name in vain, what acts do not honor your father or mother, could you ever make a movie depicting the life of Jesus? These all remind us of what living under the law was really like always, wondering if this practice was okay or not okay.

I think when you come to the rest of chapter 7, it is these endless uncertainties of the law that Paul is describing when he talks about the conflict brought by the law. I also believe this discussion will help us understand why the coming of the Holy Spirit to live inside us was so superior to the law. It is obvious that trying to live within the confines of the Ten Commandments or trying to satisfy the requirements of the law on our own is impossible. We will touch on this more in the next chapter.

There is one more part to this matter of sin that needs some attention. As we discussed earlier, Paul begins Chapter 7 talking about the marriage vow and how the only way out of a marriage relationship is the death of one of the marriage partners. Paul concludes those four verses by saying, "So my brothers, you also died to the law through the body of Christ." We have already made this point, but it needs to be said again. When you become a Christ-follower, you die to the law and you are released in the same way a marriage is dissolved when a partner dies. When you read all those verses we listed earlier in this study from Romans 6 and 7, Paul is hammering this message home. As a Christ-follower, the partnership between you and the law is over, because the law is dead, so the contract is void. You are no longer bound to the rules and regulations of that partnership.

So where does that leave us? Could it be possible that, when Paul repeatedly says the Law is "dead," he is, in essence, saying that we are back to how God dealt with His people prior to giving the law? Paul notes in Romans 5:13: "To be sure, sin was in the world before the law was given, but sin is not charged against anyone's account where there is no law."

Can we conclude from these verses that if you belong to Christ, he is not "counting" your shortcomings any more as sin? Could it be that God is not writing down in His book every mistake you have made? Paul will certainly tell us many things in his letters about how to live the Christian life. Jesus gives us in Matthew 22:37-40 the goal He wants for us: to love God above all others and to love our neighbor as ourselves. Can we accept that the Holy Spirit living in us is the best guide for living our lives? Can we accept that our willpower alone will never give us what we need to live to a set of rules? We are human beings, born with a sinful nature that will never be gone until we reach heaven. God understands this and does not expect from you what you cannot attain: PERFECTION. That is the wonder of Romans 3:21: "But now a righteousness from God apart from the law has been revealed." If you belong to Christ, can we just thank God for the new way and be grateful the old way is gone?

Verses 13-23

After that lengthy discussion on sin before and after "the law," I want to turn our attention to who Paul is describing in Romans 7:13-23. Is he describing himself before or after his Damascus Road encounter with Jesus and subsequent conversion to Christianity? Is he talking about himself as a believer or a nonbeliever? This is the question theologians and pastors cannot agree about.

I choose to believe Paul is talking about what it was like for him prior to becoming a Christian for the following reasons:

It makes sense when considering the flow of this chapter. The first group of verses in this chapter drive Paul's point home that the law is dead. The second group of verses are his response to the question, "Is the law sinful?" He says no because the purpose of the law always has been and always will be to point out our sin and point us toward Christ. In verse 13, he goes on to say that this dead law is still good because God used it to bring Paul to a place where he could recognize his need for Christ. Paul hints at this again in the second half of verse 24, when he says, "Who will rescue me from this body that is subject to death?"

I believe verse 14 begins Paul's firsthand description of his experience when he was living under the law as a Jew and a Pharisee. His descriptive and passionate words paint a frustrating picture of what it is like trying to live by a set of rules and regulations as a way of eliminating our sin. Paul lived this frustration daily. He understood what it felt like. This section of verses makes me want to cry, "Please God, is this how you want me to live as your adopted child? With all this frustration, struggle, and fear? Paul paints this picture for us to contrast the difference between living under the law and living by (or in) our faith. (The living by faith side of this contrast will come in Chapter 8).

In both verses 14 and 23 of this chapter, Paul talks of being a "slave to sin" and "a prisoner of the law of sin." But repeatedly in his writings, Paul says he is no longer a slave to sin. That is Paul, post-conversion. These verses then must be Paul referring to himself before he became a Christian. Romans 8:15 is one such verse: "The Spirit you received does not make you slaves, so that you live in fear again; rather, the Spirit you received brought about your adoption to sonship." And by him we cry, "Abba, Father."

If these verses are describing Paul as a Christian, are we to understand that every Christian will face this same frustration and struggle? Martin Luther experienced this frustration. He was caught in a vicious circle of sin, performing some sort of work to make up for that sin, another sin, another work of self-atonement, another sin, and so on. Then he read Paul's words: "The just shall live by faith," and his life was never the same. He found the peace Paul speaks of in Chapter 5:1. The "peace with God through our Lord Jesus Christ." The Paul I know would have said, "No, Martin, thank God He has delivered you just like He did me."

Another important point to consider is that this is the only place in Paul's writings that he talks with such desperation about his struggle with sin. Why don't we see anything like this anywhere else in Paul's writings? Instead, I think of Paul writing in Gal 5-1: "It is for freedom that Christ has set us free. Stand firm, then, and do not let yourselves be burdened again by a yoke of slavery." Or 2 Tim 4-7: "I have fought the good fight, I have finished the race, I have kept the faith. Now there is in store for me the crown of righteousness." In Gal 2-20: "I have been crucified with Christ and I no longer live, but Christ lives in me." These are the words of Paul I see throughout his writings. He knew of his standing with God. I refuse to believe he ever wondered if he was okay with God.

Before we move on to vs 25, we need to ask these questions of those who believe this is Paul as a Christian. How often does this occurrence that Paul describes here in chapter 7 happen? Is it daily, weekly, monthly or once a year? If this is a regular occurrence for a Christian, how can we say we have "Peace with God"?

Now we arrive at verse 25. I believe this little verse is perhaps the most compelling reason to believe this is Paul before he became a Christian. I believe verses 13-24 are describing Paul as a nonbeliever. Verse 24 is full of despair. "What a wretched man I am! Who will rescue me from this body that is subject to death?" Paul is giving words to the despair he felt when he was under the law. But then verse 25 is Paul's answer to his own question. It is an answer full of hope because it is how Paul was set free from this struggle. **"Thanks be to God, who delivers me through Jesus Christ our Lord."**

Paul is very clear here. Because of Jesus Christ there **is deliverance from this struggle.** It is not a future deliverance; Paul says it is now, it is when you become a Christ-follower. You must remember Paul's words from Romans 5-1: "Therefore, being justified by faith, I have peace with God." Paul knew that peace, it was not a future peace, it was now. Again and again, Paul would teach that peace is not contingent on your outward circumstances; it is from inside. In Philippians 4-11 he says, "I have learned to be content whatever the circumstances." I refuse to believe that Paul, after his conversion, ever wondered again, let alone on a regular basis, if he was delivered.

Finally, we need to remember that there are no chapter breaks in Paul's letter. Those were added much later. That would mean that the first verses of chapter 8 would have immediately followed Paul's statement that God has delivered him. Consider the first verse of chapter 8: "Therefore, there is no condemnation for those who are in Christ Jesus, because through Christ Jesus, the law of the Spirit who gives life has set you free from the law of sin and death." Throughout the rest of this great chapter, Paul will teach what it is like to "live in our faith" with the Holy Spirit living inside of us. This is the other side of the contrast Paul is making. Chapter 7 is what it is like before Christ, chapter 8 is what it is like to live with Christ. Chapter 8 is how Paul lived his life every day from his conversion to his death. It is how he lived through all kinds of suffering and imprisonment. It just seems impossible to me that Paul could write chapter 8 and still go back to the life he described in verses 14-24 of chapter 7.

As we conclude chapter 7, I want once again to go back to verse 4: "So, my brothers and sisters, you also died to the law through the body of Christ...." The dictionary defines the word "died" in these words: to stop living, to expire, to cease existing. Paul uses this word because it cannot be misunderstood. When you are a follower of Christ, the law stops. It ceases to exist for you. It expires, yes; it is dead. Those are Paul's words.

Paul repeats this idea over and over in the book of Romans:

Romans 3:21 - "But now apart from the law the righteousness of God has been made known...."

Romans 3:28 - "For we maintain that a person is justified by faith apart from the works of the law."

Romans 6:14 - "For sin shall no longer be your master, because you are not under the law, but under grace."

Romans 8:2 - "...the law of the Spirit who gives you life has set you free from the law of sin and death."

Romans 8:3 - "For what the law was powerless to do because it was weakened by the flesh,[b] God did by sending his own Son..."

Romans 10:4 - "Christ is the end of the law so that there may be righteousness for everyone who believes."

It seems to me that Paul is very clear on this point. The law is dead. I grew up in a church of Christians where we read the law every Sunday. Our pastors preached on each item of the Ten Commandments as separate sermons. We had our weekly "time of confession" and "assurance of pardon." This is still part of many Christian churches today. Every time I hear a pastor reading the law, or preaching on the Ten Commandments, or telling me "if" I confess then God will forgive, I wonder to myself how we can say we believe the law to be dead, when it seems so alive in our churches today? How can I have the "peace of God" Paul assures me of in Romans 5-1 if the law is still part of our Christian life today. Listen to these words of Paul in Colossians 2:13-14: "When you were dead in your sins and in the uncircumcision of your flesh, God made you alive with Christ. He forgave us all our sins, having canceled the charge of our legal indebtedness, which stood against us and condemned us; he has taken it away, nailing it to the cross." If that is true, and the church still teaches we need to live by "the law," did my sins somehow come "unnailed" from the cross? Do they only get renailed to the cross whenever I confess them?

Why is it so difficult for us to let go of the law and accept that for a Christ-follower the law is dead? Do we worry that the Holy Spirit living inside us is not adequate to keep us connected to our heavenly Father? Do we need our own willpower to assist the Holy Spirit? But then, I read Romans 8:37: "No, in all these things we are more than conquerors through him who loved us. For I am convinced that neither death nor life, neither angels nor demons, neither the present nor the future, nor any powers, neither height nor depth, nor anything else in all creation, will be able to separate us from the love of God that is in Christ Jesus our Lord." Nothing, not even our sin, Paul says, can separate us from our heavenly Father. Amen.

I suppose I must concede that there is room for both arguments to be made. There are sentences in this last section that are hard to understand if taken alone. This is why we have spent so much of this chapter talking about who Paul was writing to, how many of his arguments were in anticipation of their questions, and Paul's own story. It all plays a part in understanding this letter. We cannot take a single verse or phrase out of that context without losing the essence and intention of what he was trying to teach.

Maybe the final question should be, does God want us to live like Martin Luther with the question of "Who will deliver me?" hanging over his head? Or does God want us to live knowing that nothing "in all creation, will be able to separate us from the love of God"? The latter is the Paul I know, and it is the life I choose to live. For me it is not "who will deliver me?" Rather, I can say with Paul, "Thanks be to God, who delivers me through Jesus Christ our Lord!"

ROMANS 8

Living with the Holy Spirit: The New Way

It is hard to imagine any chapter in the Bible filled with more meaning to a Christ-follower than this eighth chapter of Romans. This chapter follows the picture Paul paints in chapter 7 of his struggle with living under the law. This chapter is Paul's final words of chapter 7 when he asks, "Who will deliver me from this struggle?" and then answers with those words, "I thank God it is through Jesus Christ."

This chapter is Paul's explanation of how Jesus has delivered him from his struggle living under the law. It is the response Paul noted in the passage from 2 Cor 5-17: "Therefore, if anyone is in Christ, they are a New creation. The 'old is gone,' the 'new has come.'" This chapter is about the "new creation" and about "the new that has come."

Verse 1 surely must be the "heart cry" of every Christ-follower. It must give a sense of joy that for many, including Martin Luther, is almost impossible to express. There is no condemnation for those who belong to Christ Jesus. Those words set us free from all our failures and Paul says it is all because you now belong to Jesus Christ. Then he goes on in verse 2 to explain why. It is because Jesus Christ, through the working of the Holy Spirit, has set you free from the law of "sin and death." In Romans 6:23, "The wages of sin is death but the gift of God is eternal life," Paul is saying that the death part of those words are gone, the gift part is now all yours because you belong to Christ. May I just remind us of a simple truth: there is no "IF" anymore in "If you confess your sins." God will forgive. Paul is saying once you belong to Christ those IF's are gone because the "law of sin brings death is gone." How could Paul be more clear than that? That is the response to his question, "Who will deliver me from this struggle with sin?" His resounding answer here in chapter 8 and verse 2 is—JESUS CHRIST.

It is almost as if Paul knows how hard this is to accept for many of us and his readers of that day that he wants to explain this truth even more.

In verses 3-4, Paul goes on to explain why these truths are valid. He begins in verse 3 by saying, "What the law could not do, God did by sending His own Son to be a sin offering." It is important to ask, what was the law not able to do? The answer is that the law probably could help us live better, it probably could help people sin less, but it could not make us PERFECT, and that is what Jesus did when he died and paid our penalty and gave His righteousness to His followers. Perfect is the only standard acceptable to God, nothing less will do. Here, we need to understand the truth of Hebrews 10 -12: "But when this priest (Jesus) had offered for all time one sacrifice for sin, He sat down at the right hand of God." Then in verse 14, the writer of Hebrews concludes by saying, "By one sacrifice He has made perfect forever." That is what the law could not do.

Then Paul concludes this teaching in verse 4 by saying, "That the righteous requirements of the law might be FULLY met in those who live with the Holy Spirit inside. "Fully" means they are all paid for, not most, not a lot of them, but "all" of them. Your sin is gone in God's eyes. There is no other way to understand Paul. The requirements of the law were fully met in Christ's sacrifice on the cross."

It almost seems impossible to imagine how Paul could have been more clear, that when you belong to Christ you are forgiven forever, not up to that point or the past, but forever. That means, throughout the future, God is not counting your sins anymore. He is asking you to serve, to bear fruit. He is saying in these four verses, "Accept that I have paid it all and set you free." Why is it so hard for us to accept God's offer and live free? Just remember again Romans 3-21: "But now a righteousness from God has been revealed that has nothing to do with the law."

Verses 5-8

Here, Paul is acknowledging that there are those who will not become Christ-followers, and he makes it clear that path does not lead to a good end. Paul must be thinking of where he was prior to his conversion and thinking how he was so sure at that point he was right. Realizing now that what seemed so right could now seem so wrong. One can only imagine the hurt Paul feels saying, how can I get them to see what I see. I think these verses are filled with that frustration and his realizing that the old way is so hard to change. His ending in verse 8, "Those who are in the flesh cannot please God," is, I think, Paul saying, failing to accept what God offers through Jesus will never end well.

Verse 9-15

Here is another set of verses filled with several truths. We must note the contrast Paul draws here between his words in chapter 7-14, "sold into bondage to sin," and 7-23 describing himself as "a prisoner to sin" with the words of these verses. Here Paul says, you as Christ-followers are not living in the old way but the new way of the Holy Spirit, and concludes in verse 15, "You are not slaves," which is the opposite of his words noted above from chapter 7.

Paul makes particular note here of the presence of the Holy Spirit in the life of every believer. He goes so far as to say if the Holy Spirit is not in you, then you are not a Christ-follower. Paul is reminding his readers of Jesus' words from John 16 -7, where He promises the coming of the Holy Spirit to live in His followers. Paul surely is testifying that from the struggle to give up on the old way in his own life noted in chapter 7 verses 14-24, that it was the Holy Spirit that changed his life and that we all need the Holy Spirit to change our hearts to become Christ-followers.

Then in verses 15b-17

Here is a truth so profound that it is hard for any Christ-follower to really comprehend. Paul teaches us that we are now adopted into God's family. As if that were not enough, he teaches that we are now heirs with Christ in our relation to the Heavenly Father. We think of what it means to be an heir of our earthly parents where it makes us recipients of the inheritance left to us by our parents. That is what Paul is saying here, we are co-heirs with Christ. We will share in the same inheritance that Christ will have in heaven. We think of the parable of the prodigal son and how the father welcomed him with a feast. That is what is in store for every Christ-follower. The three stories from Luke 15 of the three lost items all conclude with a banquet in heaven when the lost were found. That is how God rejoices when a lost person gets saved. That thought surely should motivate us to do all we can to see that lost persons living apart from God get saved.

I want to share a personal understanding of what being part of God's family really means to me. I think of my family when they were all at home sitting around the supper table talking about the day's events. The happenings at school, the issues with their friends, what a teacher may have said or done, those are some of my fondest memories of family times. Now, I try to imagine if my children would end that suppertime by saying, "Dad, I made some mistakes today. I need to know if you will forgive me and 'if' I can still be part of this family." Even writing this fills me with emotion thinking of what I would say. I know what I would want to say: "How can you even think such a thought. Don't you know you are part of this family? You belong here, nothing you do can change your belonging to this family." Then I wonder if we think belonging to God's family is less secure, that He would let go of members of His family easier than I would. Everything in me believes—and everything Paul says as he concludes this eighth chapter asking, "What can separate me from God?" and his answer over and over is nothing—no, God cares even more for His family than I ever could for mine.

Verse 17b

Paul must have been aware that many of these Christians were enduring persecution. He is telling them that suffering is part of believing in Jesus. Then in verse 18, he just wants them to know that, in the end, what they gain from being a Christ-follower will far outweigh the suffering they are going through now. I often think as American Christians we have a Westernized view of Christianity. That view is that God wants all of us to be healthy, wealthy, and happy. But that is not the state of many, many Christians today in many other countries. They know that being a Christian will bring suffering, physical harm, ostracizing, and imprisonment, and in some cases, death. Too often, our selfish wants have led to spending all our resources striving for that health, wealth, and what we think will bring happiness. Many of our Christian brothers and sisters would see life very differently. Paul considered it a privilege to suffer for Christ. We only must read 2 Cor 11 to see the extent of his suffering. We have a different philosophy that seems rather to say, if I can afford it that must mean God wants me to have it. Most of us are part of churches that cater more to our wants than the needs of our Christian brothers and sisters facing extreme circumstances we have never experienced. Persecution is very real in many places in the world and the message Paul wrote to the church at Rome could be just as applicable today. We as the church need to be made much more aware of those facing persecution.

Verses 19-21

Here, Paul teaches that even God's creation has been suffering. We think of God's words to Adam and Eve that thorns and thistles will grow and earning a living will require hard work, sweat, and tears. Since we have never seen a time that weeds did not grow, we can only imagine what Adam and Eve must have seen. From a beautiful garden with no weeds, no dead flowers or dead trees, friendly animals, no fear of being chased by a lion or mauled by a bear. For the first time, they saw their crops competing with weeds, short of water or with too much water. They saw storms come and ruin their crops and bugs eat their crops. They must have thought back to the good days when it was all different. Paul simply here wants us to recognize—and especially those suffering (which today is true for so many in the world because of their faith, but also because of what has happened to God's creation)—that someday this will end. Paul speaks of the groaning from the earth but also from His people waiting for that day to return when the earth will return to what God intended it to be.

Then as Paul ends these verses, he reminds us that we live with hope based on what we believe is coming. Paul wants to remind us that we really have no idea what will be ours when we are finally in heaven forever as part of God's family. We remember Paul's words from 1 Cor 2: "Eye hath not seen nor ear heard nor has it entered into our imagination what God has prepared for those that love Him." We need to remember Paul talking of being caught up to heaven when he was stoned so he must have had a glimpse of what was awaiting those who belong to Christ 2 Cor 12. We know of people today who have been revived from what seemed death and talk of things they saw. These stories only heighten our wonder of what is coming. Surely, this fueled Paul's passion for the gospel to see and then know some are going to miss it. That must be Paul's concern to quit living for performance and start living to bear fruit.

Verse 26-27

Here, we come to a truth that it is hard to fully grasp, but the content of these verses truly is profound for every Christ-follower. Paul is reminding us, as he did in verse 9, of the presence of the Holy Spirit living inside of every Christ-follower. Here in these verses, he tells us that the Holy Spirit living inside of us knows that every situation we are dealing with is going to God the Father and letting Him know of our needs. Can you imagine what that means because He lives with you? He really knows everything going on with you, every concern, every fear, the things that bring you great joy and the ones you just cannot find an answer to. The relationships that you cannot figure out how to fix, the doctors report you cannot get out of your mind. All those things the Holy Spirit is sharing with the God of the universe. Do you wonder what He is telling God about your life right now, down to the thoughts going through your mind even now? He knows it all. Then in the last part of verse 27, "He intercedes for the saints (that means you) according to God's will". Have you ever looked back at something you prayed for and said, "I'm sure glad God didn't answer that prayer." Paul is saying, do not worry the Holy Spirit has you covered. He knows God's plan for you. He is asking God for what is best for you. I think it still goes even further when we really understand this in the context of a bigger picture that we will see in the next verse of this chapter.

Verses 28

"And we know that in all things God works for the good of those who love Him and are called according to His purpose."

I truly believe this verse is one of the most misused verses in all the Bible. I remember a friend at one point saying, "It was hard when I had a car accident to say, 'thank you, God, for this accident.'" To that person, it was obeying this verse. Some would suggest that I should be thankful when a doctor says I have cancer, when a young mother dies leaving her children she will never see graduate from school. This is how we often seek to understand this single verse. Before we assign these events to God, we need to hear the words of James 1-13: "Let no one say when he is tempted that I am tempted by God for God cannot be tempted by evil and He does not tempt anyone."

I want to suggest, rather, that this verse needs to be part of a set of verses that really started back in verse 26 and ends with verse 39.

Paul is trying to explain God's care over those who have become part of His family. When we understand that concept, then this verse will have the meaning it was intended to have. Let us take these fourteen verses as a picture Paul wants us to see of God's love and care for his adopted children.

In the verses, we just looked at 26-27, where Paul has shared how God, through the presence of the Holy Spirit living in us, is aware of everything going on in our lives. He knows what is coming. He knows what is happening today and He knows what has happened. The Holy Spirit updates God every day relaying your needs, pains, joys, and fears. He really cares and watches out for you.

Then in verse 28, we hear Paul's words: "God causes all things to work together for good to those who love God, to those who are 'called according to His purpose.'"

Those last words—"to those called according to His purpose"—lead us into verses 29-30, where verse 30 concludes, "And those He predestined he also called; those he called he also justified; those he justified he also glorified."

Here, while on their own, clearly speak of God's intervention in us becoming part of His family. However, that is not the primary focus of these verses. Paul, responding to the "called according to His purpose" here, is saying God had a plan for your life that started in eternity and will end in eternity. That is the essence of verse 28, that God has your life in His hand, and nothing is going to change that. That is the essence of "all things will work together for good." God is not going to let anything change that. We live in a world with the consequences of sin that is reality for all of us, but God is saying I will get you through it. You may get a bad doctors report, a relationship may go bad, a storm of many sizes and shapes may affect your life but, in the end, God will bring you safely home.

Verse 31

Paul here is just saying "who is going to change God's plan for you." God gave up His only Son for your life. How would He ever let go of You? Imagine if you gave up something very precious or expensive to purchase any item? Would not what you gave away to get that item determine how hard you would hang onto it? That is Paul's argument here. God gave up His one and only Son for you and He is not going to let go of you.

Verse 33-34

Here, Paul uses another argument to make his case. He reminds us that God is the one who is the final judge no one can overrule Him. It is like the Supreme Court. They have the final say. Paul is saying, if God says you belong to Him, no one can overrule Him. You are His, you belong to Him. Never forget that.

Verse 35-39

Here, Paul begins his final defense of verse 28, "...that all things will work for my good." He does it by asking the most important question, "Who can separate me from God." Connecting it to verse 28, Paul is really saying, "Can anything keep me from attaining the result of God's plan for me, that will not be for my good?" His answer in the last verses of chapter 8 is a resounding NO.

Paul wanted all Christ-followers to know that, no matter the current suffering you may be going through, God has a plan for you. It started before you were even born, and the end was secured by Him and nothing is going to change that. I think of David when he talked of walking through the valley of the shadow of death. He said he could do it because God is walking through it with him. David knew because of that truth, the end was guaranteed. That is what Paul is saying to us, as he concludes this great chapter.

How can you read those final verses and not get choked up with emotion? Not death, not life, not governments, not the present, not the future, no earthly power. Then you sense Paul cannot find all the words he wants, so he adds words that just cover all the bases. Nothing, nothing, nothing can keep me from the future with my heavenly Father. Then I remember Jesus saying, "I'm going to prepare a place for you." Would He do that if there was a chance you would not be coming?"

This is how we need to see the real meaning of verse 28:

Verse 26-27

The Holy Spirit is connecting you to your Heavenly Father. He knows everything going on with you.

Verse 29-30

God has a life all planned out for you. It started before you were born and it will end in heaven when it has done.

Verse 31-34

God is the final judge. He loves you and has adopted you into His family. He gave His only Son up for you and you can be sure He will not give you up ever.

Verse 35-39

No one, not anything, can take you out of God's hand.

As we conclude this special chapter of the Bible, Paul has taught us in several different ways what it means to belong to His family. No matter how much we talk about this chapter, it is hard to do justice to all that is contained in it.

There is one final thought that needs to be clear that really goes to the heart of all that Paul has written in this chapter. It is the words from verse one: "There is no condemnation to those who are in Christ.". All the blessings contained in this chapter hinge on that single prerequisite that "you are in Christ, that you belong to His family." That is the truth contained in a verse familiar to almost every person exposed to the Bible, John 3-16: "For God so loved the world that He gave His only son that whoever 'BELIEVES' in Him shall not perish but have eternal life." Then the next verse John 3-18: "He who believes in Him is not judged; he who does not believe has been judged already." These not-so-familiar words remind us of the consequences of rejecting the gospel. That is why Paul prefaces it all by saying, "There is no judgement, no condemnation for those who are IN CHRIST." To all those who would teach multiple ways to God, surely, these words must cause you great concern. To all those who would teach that God judges based on performance, these words must challenge you. To all who want to make being right with God a matter of their way, need to hear these words.

Paul could not be more clear as he writes this chapter of Romans. Our eternal destiny depends on this relationship with Jesus Christ. The way is clear, the consequences are enormous, and Jesus is that way He is the only way. Paul's description in this chapter of living as part of God's family can bring us the only peace that is not dependent on the circumstances of this life.

If you have never joined God's family, I hope you will accept God's offer and do it today as you finish this chapter.

ROMANS 9

Struggling with Election

It is hard to imagine any chapter of the Bible that has caused more disagreement among Christians and non-Christians than this chapter. The words that Paul quotes, "Jacob have I loved but Esau have I hated,"' surely rank among the most controversial words in the Bible. They stand in contrast to some of Jesus' most memorable words of John 3-16: "For God so loved the world." Which imply and are understood to mean God loves all people.

So, the question is, how do we understand this chapter?

I want to suggest that here is a classic example of where we need to understand the context that causes Paul to write these words. The first five verses of this chapter give us the heart of Paul for the Jewish people and their rich history. We have discussed in other places in Romans the unbelievably difficult task Paul faced to change the Jewish people's understanding (Paul's family) of the change Christ has brought. Paul has seen just how wrong this rich history has been in understanding God's redemptive plan for the world. You sense his emotion as he says, I would give up my place in God's family to see my Jewish family change course and embrace Christ.

I choose to believe that it was Paul's own experience that brought him to faith that impacts so much of these next three chapters. Paul knew of his own resistance to the gospel. He had to have thought of all those new Christians he had delivered to a prison and some to their death. He knew that even seeing the faith commitment of those Christians could not convince him that this new "way" (the gospel) that had impacted their lives was worth considering. He knew that only one thing could have changed him and that was Jesus' intervention on that trip to Damascus. Nothing could have been more clear to him than that. God chose to change him. How could that not have made him try to deal with that reality? It surely is why this chapter is here at all.

We have seen the debate over this chapter throughout the history of the church. Calvinists are thought to be the originator of the doctrine of "unconditional election," but in reality, it is the Apostle Paul. It is this chapter. No matter how many sermons we have heard preached, none have solved the mystery contained in this chapter.

Dr. Barnhouse, in one of his books, reminds us of how God is involved in all kinds of choosing in our lives. He ends by saying, "Please God, do not leave the choice to go to heaven up to me, for Romans 3-10 says, 'There is none righteous, not even one, no one who understands and no one who seeks God.'" Dr. Barnhouse was convinced that, if the choice were left to him, he would not choose God.

The mystery of this, we will see, challenged Paul just as it challenges us. When this chapter is done, we will still face the mystery. We know its reality but not how it works.

At the heart of this chapter is Paul seeing so many of his Jewish family rejecting Christ. It is his attempt to explain this rejection that prompts all the arguments he makes in chapter 9. If we are to have any hope of understanding this chapter, that must be our starting point.

Some of the truths Paul is teaching in this chapter surely had repercussions in his day, but surely, they need to be heard throughout the church today. Those truths are so prominent in the verses 6-8. These words must have reverberated through every Jewish community and, surely, within the Christian Jewish community, as well. Let us just highlight them:

1. Verse 6: Paul says just because you are of Jewish descent does not make you part of Israel in God's plan.

2. Verse 7: Paul says just because you are Jewish does not mean you are a descendent of Abraham in God's plan.

3. Verse 8: Paul says it is not the natural born Jewish children who are God's children, but the children of the promise (God's promise to Abraham that Sarah would have a child) that are really God's children.

It is impossible for us to imagine how these words of Paul must have stung the ears of so many Jewish people who had never known anything except that they were God's chosen people.

We must understand that this is the basis Paul is using to understand why so many of his people have rejected the gospel. He wants us to understand that, way back when God interacted with Abraham, "choice" was already part of God's plan. This is what leads Paul on in this chapter 9 to try to explain and to justify God's choosing. It would seem reasonable for us to acknowledge the hazard Paul faced going down that road. I think of Jesus' words to His disciples in John 15-19: "Because I have chosen you out of the world the world will hate you." That is the path Paul is on, as he moves to the verses that follow in Chapter 9.

Before we go further, I think we need to say more about the issue Paul has opened in verses 6-8. If you are familiar with all the preaching related to Israel and its future and the role so many see between America and Israel, then these words at least need to be carefully looked at and they must become part of those discussions. Paul could not be more clear stating that just being of Jewish ancestry does not make you part of God's family. Paul will teach over and over through his letters that you only come to God's family through accepting Jesus Christ as your personal Savior. You do not come by nationality. All God's family must come today through Christ.

So, moving on to the rest of this chapter, we come to verses 10-13. Here, we find the words that have troubled so many for so long—"Jacob have I loved but Esau I have hated"—words first spoken by the prophet in Malachi 1:2-3. Paul is continuing his explanation of why some of the Jewish people have rejected Christ and the gospel he has been preaching.

Paul is trying to explain that God has always been involved in choosing. He begins in these verses by using the choice God made to use one of Issac's children, Jacob, and not another son, Esau. I want to be clear that I am not a scholar of Greek or Hebrew, as I share these thoughts about this chapter. I just have this feeling that the words here of love versus hate are translated words that really mean to be, chosen versus to not be chosen. Gen 25 verse 23 concludes talking about this relationship of Jacob and Esau, saying, "and the older will serve the younger." Perhaps, this is a better context than our definition of love versus hate.

We forget that God has always been involved in choosing. He chose Abraham over Lot to be the father of the nation of Israel. He chose Moses over all the babies that were killed to lead His people out of Egypt. He chose Pharaoh to be the king that Moses would confront and show God's power. He chose David out of eight siblings to be the king of Israel. He chose Matthew out of all the tax collectors to go to his house for dinner. He chose twelve disciples out of all the people He could have chosen. He chose one of the short people, Zacchaeus, and stopped at his tree and said, "I am coming to your house not to your neighbor's house." He chose one crippled man at the pool of Siloam, passing by many that needed help, and healed just the one. God chose Mary to carry His Son Jesus out of all the women He could have chosen, and He chose Joseph, a carpenter, to be Mary's husband. And yes, He chose Paul out of all the obstinate Pharisees to write this letter we call the constitution of the Christian faith.

God is involved in choosing and that is at the heart of what Paul is trying to explain in these verses. Paul does not say, nor should we, that any of the people God passed over in His choice were lost for eternity. We do not know about the fate of Esau, Lot, or David's eleven brothers, or perhaps even Pharaoh. We only know for sure that God did not choose them for the task He wanted done. We do know that God makes all kinds of choices in our lives. Psalm 139 tells us that God formed all of us, so if you are five-feet, eight-inches tall you will not be a center in the NBA. If you are thin and weigh 150 pounds, you will not be a lineman in the NFL and that was God's choosing.

We do know that it is this passage that has led theologians to develop doctrines like Reprobation that have created so much resentment. Paul will teach us here in Chapter 9, I think, that there are mysteries about God's dealings that we will never understand. When we add our human logic to God's ways, we often find that they lead us to human conclusions, which do not match the God we saw in Chapter 8. We do know that God is God. He can choose, and He does choose no matter how we choose to describe His choosing.

Verses 14-15

Here, Paul raises a question he knows will result from his teaching—"Does this make God unjust?" Surely, it is a logical question Paul knows is in the minds of those reading this letter.

Verse 19

This is a verse that reflects another question Paul knows is in the mind of his readers—"Why does God still blame us?" To our human understanding that seems a logical question to ask.

Reading this chapter is still a troubling chapter for many Christians today. It stands in contrast to the words of Jesus we all have memorized, John 3-16: "For God so loved the world."

Verse 20

This verse, "Who are you o man to talk back to God?" may teach us that trying to explain some of these mysteries by human logic can only lead us down a path that does not have a good ending.

We sense that Paul is feeling his own inadequacy to explain this mystery in the words, "Who are you to talk back to God?" The reality is that Paul has raised the question in verses 14 and 19. He knows there are no human answers to adequately explain these mysteries. Verses 21-23 are Paul's continuing attempt to explain by asking, "Does not the Maker have the right to make each of us as He wants?" But he cannot escape his questions from 14 and 19 that imply from a human perspective "no." That would seem to us unfair.

I cannot help but wonder if Paul ever regretted writing these words. The consequence of this choosing is about eternity, not about a potential position on a football or basketball team. We know the argument that, in Adam, we all died. So Paul proposes here—"does not God have the right out of all those lost people to save some? That at least, to our minds, is a more plausible answer. Paul implies in verse 18 that God shows His mercy by this choosing. Then for the verses 25- 29, Paul uses various passages from the Bible to show that choosing has always been a part of God's dealings with people. We have already discussed that, and we know that is true.

I am reminded of a trip I took to India. We visited an ancient city on the Ganges river and, early one morning, we floated down the river and saw cremation fires burning along the shore with the smoke and the smell hanging over the river as we floated along. We learned that it was the Hindu belief that, if within twenty-four hours of death you could be cremated, and your ashes spread in the Ganges river, you could bypass some of the reincarnation steps after death. I realized that, for centuries, this had been their practice, the only religion they had ever known from a child to death. I saw firsthand the poverty they live in. That morning, early as we drove to the river, I saw children digging through piles of garbage for food. Most of them will never hear the gospel ever. At the end of that trip, we sat to reflect on what we had seen and experienced, and I still remember my thoughts. Why do I get to be born in a Christian home in America going to church twice every Sunday, hearing the gospel over and over, and never having to search for food? Why me? Why was I not born in India? All I know is that I had nothing to do with any of this. It is all God's doing. All I could say, or think is, "Thank you, God." And all I can do now is to help get the gospel to those who have never heard it. I think that Paul's goal in all this is to remind us that, if you are one of God's children, if you have been adopted into God's family, you ought to be so grateful, certainly not proud. I think Paul knew it was that sense of gratitude that changed him and that it could also change us.

This chapter is the primary basis for so much division in the different denominations that have developed since the reformation. We divide ourselves whether we have a free will or not and how we present the gospel. If one reads Ephesians 2 (8-9) where Paul clearly talks of faith as a "gift," then how can we imply that faith is a matter of "one's will power"? And if so, then surely it opens the door to my boasting. Paul has said clearly in chapter 4 that boasting is excluded.

We all seem to agree that we cannot argue anyone into the kingdom of heaven. We agree that is the work of the Holy Spirit. Our task must be to share the good news. I think Paul could not adequately explain the mystery of why some will respond to the gospel and some will not, and neither can we. Jesus said that, "Whoever believes in me will not be lost" (John 3-16). Jesus also said, "Behold I stand at the door and knock, if anyone hears my voice and opens the door, I will come into him" (Rev 3-20). It seems that should be the message we all could accept and share with the world and leave the rest to God. Can we take note of Jesus' words in Rev 3-20 when he says whoever "hears my voice" and be reminded that people need to hear the gospel to respond? We will see that again in chapter 10. Nothing should challenge the church more than that the call of Jesus when He said, "Go into all the world and preach the gospel to every person."

Paul concluded this chapter with verses 30-33. Here, he reminds his readers that pursuing eternity in heaven by trying to be good will not work. He says again it only happens by giving up and trusting Christ to make you perfect and free of sin. His message here is the same, it is not your nationality that gets you to heaven. It is what you believe. Believing you are a sinner who needs a Savior and asking Jesus to be your Savior to pay for your sin is the only way to set you free to bear fruit for Him.

Final Thoughts That I Want to Leave

The reality of God choosing cannot be denied and, in the end, God is God. What He chooses to do will not be changed whether that choosing aligns with my sense of justice. The Bible, as we have discussed, is clear that God's ways are greater than our ways, His thoughts above ours. I see no practical application of this mystery in our work as individuals or as the church of Christ. I have never met any person who wanted desperately to follow Christ but just said Jesus is not letting me in. But I have met those who said this Christianity just does not make sense to them. Those are the people that I struggle with, and I know that it is the work of the Holy Spirit. I wonder, why He does not push harder. In the end, that is God's part not mine.

There are those who have used this chapter to decide not to do missions because telling unelected people about the gospel would only increase their punishment in eternity. I cannot even imagine how revolting that would have been to Paul. Paul's ministry was to go to every venue he could find to share the gospel. Everywhere he went, he shared the gospel without any indication of reluctance. He faced suffering because of his unashamed preaching of the gospel. You must hear him say, "Woe is me if I do not preach the gospel." Paul knew that God called him to bring the gospel to the world. The calling, however it works, was God's part, not his, and surely that must be our and the churches' thinking today.

Jesus said in Rev 3-20: "I stand at the door and knock; if anyone hears My voice and opens the door, I will come into them and will dine with them and they with me." We need to be very clear to all who have used these words of Paul as an excuse for not believing or doing mission work. There is no one standing at the door to Jesus knocking that Jesus does not open the door to. If you have any nudging of your heart to explore Christianity, that is the Holy Spirit at work. He is pushing you to open the door of your heart to the message that Jesus died for you and wants to forgive you.

For a number of years, I was involved in a program called Evangelism Explosion, where we actively visit people with the intent to share the gospel in a way Peter reminded us in 1 Peter 3-15: with gentleness and respect. I have witnessed that the same presentation of the gospel that has no impact on one can have the opposite effect on another. We know the stories of people invited to a Billy Graham crusade who only went to not offend the person asking them to go. Those people tell of feeling a sense of being compelled to go forward at the end of the service to accept Christ.

Jesus said go into "All the World" and preach the gospel, not part of the world, but all of it. That is the task, and the rest we leave for God. Paul is our example. No matter what he said about God's choosing, it did not hinder Paul from going anywhere. People were willing to listen to the story of his changed life that he believed was available to any who would believe it.

ROMANS 10

Confess and Believe and You Are Saved

Paul begins chapter 10 by expressing some of the same thoughts as he did starting chapter 9. We can only assume how much the rejection by so many of his Jewish friends must have affected him. We assume that Paul, in his prior role, as a Pharisee, had many friends that now looked at him as their enemy. Paul begins this chapter by indicating he continues to pray for his friends that something will bring them to faith in Christ and so be saved. You can sense Paul saying, "What else can I do? What argument can I make that will convince my Jewish friends to change direction?" Early in this chapter, Paul will teach us some very important lessons.

In verse 2, Paul reminds all his readers that being zealous for God is not enough. There are those who would teach that it is not so important what you believe but that you believe in something. Paul says no, that his Jewish friend's zeal is misplaced. That it is not based in the truth. We know of so many religions that have zealous followers. They often require harsh rules and regulations to be followed, but Paul says no. There is only one way and that is by giving up and trusting Jesus Christ.

Verses 3

Paul here will repeat what he has taught throughout this book of Romans. Two things stand out in these verses:

1. The Jews are rejecting God's offer of forgiveness and the offer of Jesus to transfer His righteousness to them. We remember Paul's words from Romans 3-21, "But now a righteousness from God has been revealed." But in essence they said we do not need it.

2. The last part of verse 4 says "they sought to establish their own." This highlights for us again the distorted view of the law as understood by the Pharisees. That was how they came to a point of saying we are keeping the law so Jesus we really do not need your righteousness we have it already.

Verse 4

Here, Paul restates again what he has said over and over: the law is gone for Christ-followers. We can remember from chapter 7 where Paul said, "You died to the law."

Here, in this verse, Paul says it another way: "Christ is the end of the law." We can only assume when he says this over and over, he knew it was hard to accept that the law is dead. Here, he puts it so simply the law is done because of Christ. It still makes me wonder today what about "dead" that is not clear.

Verses 5-8

Paul uses Moses' words to say, if you are going to gain righteousness that God will accept, the standard is perfection. Not a single sin. It is not how many sins. It is just one that keeps you from a relationship with God. Then, as Paul concludes these verses, his whole argument becomes Jesus' offer is right in front of you. You do not need to search for it. Jesus' story is still fresh. He died. He rose again and He offers you His perfection. His concluding words from verse 8 will lead us to the famous words of Verse 9. He simply says it is about your mouth, it is about your heart. That is what God wants. It is not about you trying hard to be good. It is about a faith relationship that affects what you are willing to confess with your mouth and believe with your heart. Now we can understand the content of verse 9 that means everything to millions around the world.

Verse 9

This verse has surely touched the hearts of Christians all around the world. "If you confess with your mouth the Lord Jesus and believe in your heart that God raised Him from the dead, you will be saved."

The simplicity of this verse and the promise it contains surely make it one of the great verses of the Bible. When one considers all the additions various churches have added to this simple verse, it makes us wonder what Paul would say about our version of the gospel today. Surely, Paul uses simple language because he has just said, "It's near you, it's as close as your mouth, and it just needs to touch your heart." I like to think that Paul is really focused on three things when he writes this blueprint for being right with God.

1. When Paul says, if you confess the Lord Jesus, he is really asking for much more than it may seem. To confess Christ, Paul tells us to accept He is "God's Son." That Jesus left Heaven to come to earth to die for us. That He is the promised Messiah, His coming foretold by all the prophets. Jesus' words, "I and the Father are one," that is the Jesus that Paul is saying you need to confess. Not who you want Jesus to be, or any limited version of Jesus will not do. You must confess Jesus as "your Lord and Savior." That acknowledgement of Savior acknowledges I am a sinner that needs a Savior. To confess Him as Lord is to say there is no other Lord in my life. That is my confession.

2. Paul, in this verse, reminds all would-be followers that Jesus is the risen Savior. That He actually did rise

from the dead. Paul would have known it was that truth that changed the disciples and changed him when Jesus confronted him on the road to Damascus. No truth is more fundamental to the Christian faith than the resurrection. Paul's words from 1 Cor 15 say it all: "If Christ has not been raised, then our faith is worthless." Can you even imagine if you were in any way connected to the events of the crucifixion of Jesus? To now have to acknowledge the reality of the resurrection must have brought remorse, but even more a wonder at how you could have been so wrong. Paul knew some of that feeling, but he still reminds us in this verse that to deny the resurrection is to put you outside of a relationship with God.

3. To confess Jesus as your Lord and to believe (have faith) that Jesus arose from the dead is what Paul puts in front of the Jews. You sense Paul's passion speaking to his fellow Jews saying, it is so close to you. Jesus made it so simple; "just give up and trust Jesus."

Finally, before we leave this verse, we need to make one final point. This point is directed to all preachers who have figured out the exact future of Israel and use these three chapters to show that Israel still has a future in God's redemptive plan. First, I want to acknowledge that they just may be right. However, if those teachings lead the current Jews to say that I will be okay even if I reject the heart of the gospel, the person of Jesus Christ and

His resurrection, then I belive those teachings will do harm instead of good.

Let us consider the following:

Verse 9 says "IF" you confess, you will be saved. Paul, I am convinced, would also turn that around and say "IF" you do not confess, you will not be saved. That is what Jesus taught in John 3 -18 and again in John 3-36: "Whoever believes in the SON has eternal life, but whoever rejects the Son will not see life, for God's wrath remains on him."

I believe Paul and Jesus teach us that no group will come to Heaven by nationality; they must come individually by faith in Jesus Christ.

If at some point, as some teach from these chapters and particularly chapter 11-11 and 11-26, when enough Gentiles have believed, then God will save the Jews, then the question is—which Jews? Do the ones who have died up to that time having rejected the gospel get saved or do only the ones who come to faith from that point on get saved?

Last on this subject, I need to say if God chooses at some point to save all the Jews, HE is God and nothing I say will limit God. I just think we need to teach what Paul and Jesus both teach here in chapter 10- 9, and, as we have indicated, Jesus' words from John chapter 3, that to pass into eternity rejecting Christ is to be lost for eternity. Any other teaching, I believe, can give a false sense of hope to any Jew (or any person) who passes into eternity having rejected Christ.

I believe these four thoughts are all contained in Paul's words from verse 9: "If you confess with your mouth that 'Jesus is Lord' and believe in your heart that God raised Him from the dead, you will be saved." That is the simple message of the gospel. It can bring assurance and real peace to those who claim it as their own, but it is also a great warning to those who reject it.

Verse 10-14

In these verses, Paul will expand his teaching embodied in the words of verse 9.

You believe with your heart that only God can know. He knows what you really believe. You cannot fool God. Perhaps, Paul wants us to understand that the first step is to believe, then you can speak about your change. Speaking confirms what you feel inside and then you can know that you are a part of God's family and say yes, "I am saved." It is the words that come out of your mouth that tell the world who you really have transferred your trust to. Jesus spoke similar words in Matthew 10 (32-33): "Therefore everyone who confesses Me before men I will confess before my Father in Heaven." Paul is saying, you cannot keep silent. You must be willing to say to the world, "I believe." Jesus said "you are my witnesses." It was not a choice. Paul is just saying here what you say, what comes out of your mouth will confirm if you are really part of God's family.

Paul reminds us again that this gospel is for all the world. No one is left out. He reminds us the same God is the Lord of all Jews and Gentiles. He goes even further in his appeal to his Jewish family that God promises a blessing to all who confess Him as Lord. There is no difference in God's sight between Jew and Gentile. Paul surely understood how difficult that was for Jews to hear but how great for all the rest to hear.

Finally, Paul will say again in verse 13, "Everyone who calls on the name of the Lord will be saved." Paul is not teaching any conditions about election. His message is not complicated. "If you confess (call on God), He will hear and welcome you into his family." These are the words of Jesus in Luke 15, where He tells the story of the lost sheep, the lost coin, and the lost son. The story of the Prodigal son reminds us that no matter the past, God cares about you now. In all those three stories, Jesus tells of a huge banquet in heaven for every lost person who believes and confesses him as their Lord and Savior.

It must make us wonder through all the different denominations today—have we made the path to God more difficult? One can hear the words of some doubters or searchers saying, "All your different denominations tell me you don't all agree or know for sure the true path to God, so how can I?"

Paul had to struggle with his own people who wanted to stay with a path that was so difficult. A path he knew well and a path he knew was the wrong path, through all the rules and regulations of the Jewish faith. He must have thought—why do you want to keep on when Jesus has done it all for you and just asks you to accept His payment so you can become part of His family? That must have been in Paul's mind, as he started writing Romans chapter 9. Then, as he started writing, one thought led to another.

Verse 14-15

Can I paraphrase these verses?

How can they call on anyone they have never believed in?

How can they believe in one of whom they have never heard?

How can they hear without someone preaching to them?

How can they preach unless someone will send them?

We cannot leave chapter 10 without considering these words of verses 14 and 15. They form the basis for so much mission work that has been done. They certainly are a challenge to every person who professes to be a Christ-follower. No one is left out of the challenge that is contained in these verses. I can only assume Paul used these words in many places and churches where he went to speak. They are the heart of the mission effort and they contain so much passion for everyone to hear the gospel. To any person or any church that would limit sharing the gospel anywhere in the world because of some view of election, these words from Paul would say, no, never.

Here, he makes plain that all must have the chance to hear the good news. Paul knew eternity was at stake. It is as though Paul were begging all his readers to understand. This is our task, this is what God asks us to do. Never would Paul have accepted any reason to withhold sharing the gospel. I cannot imagine the look on Paul's face if anyone would have suggested that we limit the telling of the good news. Rather, Paul brings it all down to one final act that must affect all of us when he says, "How shall they preach unless they are sent?"

Paul understood that, for most of us, that is the way to be involved in Jesus' command to go and preach the gospel to the world. It is a challenge that every church needs to embrace. That is what Christians need, to hear the call to be a sender. When Paul concludes by saying, "How beautiful are the feet of those who bring good news," he is not just referring to the person who was sent. He is clearly saying that, when you are a sender, you are an integral part of bringing that good news.

Verses 16-17

"Faith comes by hearing the word of God."

Here again is a fundamental truth that has a direct impact on how we decide to be involved in bringing the good news. Paul acknowledges in verse 16 that many will not respond to the gospel. Paul, however, makes such a critical statement, when in verse 17, he writes, "Faith comes by hearing the message (good news) and that message is heard through the Word of Christ." This truth is so fundamental to all our mission work.

Paul is saying you must hear the gospel before conversion can happen. Faith does not come in the night where you go to sleep an unbeliever and wake up a Christian never having heard the gospel. Paul in Romans chapter 1 reminds us that God has shown Himself in creation. We call that general revelation. It is, however, the special revelation found in the Bible that is needed to know Christ and His offer of salvation. That is what Paul is saying, you must hear the gospel before you can respond to its message.

That must be our motivation, to reach out with the gospel. People need to hear it to accept it. You can live the best life in practice and, hopefully, it may cause people to ask what you believe, but a good life does not tell about Jesus' offer of forgiveness. Paul has just reminded us that it is "when you confess Christ and believe in His resurrection that you will be saved." That is what is needed to tell that story, and then, it is the Holy Spirit who can bring the change needed. Lost people need to hear about Christ. That is what God is asking of each of us who are His followers.

A great mission pastor I knew used to tell an imaginary story that reminded me of this truth. His story was an encounter between God and Satan. Satan asks God, "How are you going to get your message out to the world?" God says, "My people will tell my story." Satan pushes and says, "What if they do not?" God replies, "I am sure they will." Satan pushes once more and says, "Just suppose they don't." And God says, "I don't have any other plan."

That is the reality of what Paul is teaching in verses 14-15 when he questions, how they can believe something they have not heard. How can they hear unless someone tells them? How can they go and tell unless we are willing to help send them?

Verses 18-21

Here, Paul goes back again to Israel's rejection of the gospel. He reminds them of all the prophetic words spoken about the coming of a Messiah. Paul reminds them that God has never quit seeking, that He has appealed to them in so many ways. He implies that God has even tried to make Israel envious by opening this message up to others, but even that did not work. He concludes in verse 21 by saying, "All day long I have reached out to you but you have refused to listen."

We can only wonder how many times Paul must have thought, "That was me, I was where so many of you are now only even more opposed." That is, until he heard directly from Jesus and was converted. It was hearing from Jesus that changed his life, so he can say with all his passion: "Faith comes by hearing." That is why he gave his life to telling that story. Surely, he expected no less from us. Telling and sending, that is ours to do.

ROMANS 11

The Meaning of All Israel

This chapter is certainly one of the more difficult chapters to really understand. My sense is that if ten pastors used this chapter for a sermon, there would be as many interpretations of the content of this chapter. Some will use it to predict the future of Israel as a nation. Many will teach that, at some future time, the verses 11 and 25-26 say that Israel as a nation will be restored to a place of prominence again. Perhaps, they are right. But I choose not to try and predict the future of God's dealings with the nation of Israel.

It is clear from chapters 9 and 10 how Paul hurts for his people. Those two chapters and this chapter are devoted, in a large way, to his concern for the Jews. The opening question from Paul is, "Has God rejected His people." I think if Paul gave a simple answer, it would be: "No, His people have rejected Him."

Paul makes several assertions over the course of this chapter that raise questions that are hard for us to answer.

In verse 8 and again in verses 28-29, Paul teaches what seems a clear picture of God's seeming involvement in the Jews rejection of Christ. Clearly, this is consistent with some of Jesus' words when he was confronted by religious leaders who opposed his earthly ministry. John 12-40 records words from Isiah that are very harsh towards Israel. In Matthew 13-15, Jesus talks of their hearts that have grown dull to the truth. Just as we studied earlier about God choosing Isaac over Ismael, or choosing Joseph over his brothers, or David over his brothers, Paul understood that God is clearly involved in our future. All throughout Israel's history, God warned that, if they rejected Him, He would reject them. That truth surely impacted Paul's understanding of God's dealing with the Jewish people.

Verses 1-6

Paul begins this chapter with a question he knows his readers are asking—"Did God reject Israel?" Paul answers it by the example of Elijah, when he thought he was the only one left believing in God. God showed him that there were 7,000 other believers. He was not alone.

Paul could have remembered the sermon Peter preached at Pentecost. There, speaking to his fellow Jews in Acts 2-14, at the end of his sermon, 3,000 believed in God. Surely, many of these were Jews. Paul had seen in James' church in Jerusalem that thousands of Jews were turning to Christ, even if they had not rejected the Jewish laws (Acts 21-20). Surely, in Paul's preaching, he saw many Jews believing in Christ. It is important to note here that Paul's illustration of Elijah notes that there were 7,000 who were still "believers." It was the act of "believing" that God noted, not their nationality.

I think we can assume that much of Paul's teaching about those who rejected the gospel was directed at the religious leaders, the Pharisees. The change to becoming a Christ-follower surely was harder for those who were leading the religious establishment. For them, to change was to acknowledge that what they had taught for so long was wrong. To preach about a coming Messiah for generations and then, not only miss but kill that Messiah when he came, would be hard for any of us to own.

In verse 7

Paul seems to replace his usual word of election with grace. Grace here to Paul was the opposite of works. Grace was God opening the ears of Jews to the hope of the gospel. The words at the end of verse 7 and verses 8-10 are harder for us to hear. Paul speaks and goes on to explain a hardening of Jews to the gospel, that he implies is God's doing. I am reminded of Jesus' words to some of the religious critics when He told them that their hearts were hardened to ever believe His message.

Verses 11-24

Here, in these several verses, Paul is again answering a question he knows his readers are asking: "Have they fallen beyond recovery." Paul answers that with a "not at all." That response can only mean this election (grace) is not the election as we think to imply finality. Paul explains this hardening as a time for the gospel to be shared with the world (Gentiles).

There are these places where we must wonder how to read Paul correctly. Is Paul here prophesying about the future of Israel? That is how many will interpret these verses. Or is Paul sharing the hurt he feels for his people as a nation? Do these verses really share a hope rather than a prediction Paul has for his people? I choose not to draw far-reaching conclusions from single verses, which I believe lead us to places we really ought to leave to God. We discussed the content of verse 11 in our last chapter, as we looked at the ninth verse of chapter 10.

I choose to believe the latter is true. I'm reminded of Paul's words from 1 Cor 7 verse 12 or verse 25, where Paul says, "I'm speaking not the Lord." Paul, in many verses of chapter 11, shares what I believe is a personal explanation, perhaps, more of a hope about complex issues with Israel and the role they played and are playing and, maybe, will play in God's plan of redemption.

I am reminded of the events of Jesus' ascension into heaven when the angels said, "It is not for you to know the times or seasons." There are some details of the coming events that God seems to have chosen not to share with us for now, perhaps, not even with Paul.

Paul was looking through a glass, darkly seeing all the events happening. Surely, he understood clearly that God had opened the door to the world to share in His offer of eternal life with Him. Surely, watching his own people reject the Messiah was heart-wrenching for him. It seems reasonable that Paul would have struggled to explain this mystery, what it meant then, what it would mean for the future, but always with a hope for his people, the Jews.

Verses 28-32

This is an interesting part of Paul's teaching. It seems that Paul is saying that the Jews disobedience is what can open them to God's grace. It is kind of like the early chapters of Romans, where Paul leads his readers to a point where they all can see their guilt in order that they finally look for a cure. Can it be that Paul talks of an envy in verse 14? That he thinks it will cause the Jews, seeing God's blessing on the Gentiles, to turn to this true faith?

In that verse 14, Paul says he hopes that this envy will bring about the salvation of the Jews.

I get the sense that much of this chapter 11 is Paul "hoping" for a good result, looking for any possibility that may bring change to his people.

Verses 33-36

These verses lend credence, I think, to the previous thought of Paul "hoping." Here, in poetic language, Paul acknowledges what the Psalmist wrote, "Your ways are not my ways, says the Lord." Paul openly acknowledges that God's ways are far above us and often hard for us to understand.

There are some clear truths that Paul teaches here and elsewhere that must guide our understanding of the issues around Israel and whatever lies in their future. I think it would do us all good to be reminded of those truths.

1. In this chapter and verse 26, "all Israel" must be understood considering Paul's prior words, that a true Israelite in God's sight is not by nationality but by faith, one who accepts Christ. So, all Israel is really all who, by faith, have accepted Christ as their Lord and Savior.

2. Never does Paul suggest that any person, Jew or Gentile, can become right with God while rejecting His Son

Jesus Christ. We cannot teach that, somehow, Israel will be restored if they reject Christ. That is the essence of the gospel. 3. When verses like verse 25 talk of a hardening of Israel until the Gentiles get saved, we must see these as just a reality Paul sees: that the Jews have resisted Christ when they should have been the first to see.

The chapters 9-10 and 11 are difficult chapters. They contain great truths; they also contain difficult truths that will remain mysteries until Jesus returns. Paul was a Jew who was changed from being the staunchest critic of Christianity to its greatest advocate. Paul knew it was all God's doing. Now, he looks at his fellow Jews rejecting Christ as he did, and trying to understand it all. I respect those great preachers and teachers who have used these passages to predict the future of Israel. I just choose to teach that "if" you confess Christ, you will be saved, and "if" you reject Christ, you will not be saved. That is the central message of the Bible and I will leave the rest to God.

ROMANS 12

How to Know the Will of God

I choose to include these first eight verses of chapter 12 in this study because they start with the words "therefore."

We know the book of Romans is not all divided in chapters as we have it today. I wonder if this section was one that was headed by "Conclusion;" if this was Paul's final words before he goes on to discuss many practical lessons for the churches.

I think Paul wants us to go back over what we have learned in these chapters. We started out saying from the first chapter that Paul wanted in this letter to teach us how to "live in our faith." He wanted us to know that the payment Jesus made for each of us was adequate. He paid it all. My debt of sin has been replaced by Jesus' perfection. Chapter 8 is where Paul describes what is available for all who accept His offer. He wants you to sit at His table along with His one and only Son Jesus. That is His offer. He says, do not sell my offer short, do not question your adoption, you belong because He paid for you with His death on the cross. It cost Jesus everything. We should never sell short the sacrifice Jesus paid by limiting the effect to every Christ-follower. Jesus paid the "full" price for all your sin. He just asks you to accept his offer and live your life to bear fruit for Him.

That is the "therefore" Paul starts chapter 12 with.

I think what Paul was saying in these first eight verses of Chapter 12 is, "Based on all I have been teaching you, this is what I hope you will do. This is my blueprint for how to 'live in your faith.'"

Then Paul lists three things he hopes will be the result of reading this letter. He concludes these eight verses by saying, if you follow these instructions, you will be able to know God's will for you. Isn't that what all of us long for? When you come to those forks in the road of life, how do I know what God wants me to do? This is Paul's formula of how to know God's will.

Here are the 3 steps of that blueprint:

1. Paul appeals to each of us to offer ourselves to God as living sacrifices - Every Jewish person knew what a sacrifice was. It involved an animal killed and then offered up as an offering to God. That is the image Paul uses here with one exception: our sacrifice. Paul is saying it is a "living" sacrifice, a living offering to God. The first criteria to knowing God's will is to get rid of what I want to be able to say, God I am Yours. I want what You want for me. I will go where You want me to go. I will give my life to what You want. I belong to You, my life is Yours. That is what Paul is saying, which needs to be the "cry of my heart." It is not what will make me rich, famous, or popular. It is trying with all my heart to say God I am yours and really meaning it.

2. The second requirement to know the will of God, Paul says, is "don't conform to the world" - The idea that God wants me to be healthy, wealthy, and happy must be replaced by, "God, what do you want for me?" We are faced every day with advertisements suggesting the opposite. They tell us we deserve the biggest tv, the fanciest car, the biggest house and, surely, the best vacations and the latest toys. The world will tell us, it is all about me and what will make me happy. Paul says, no, Jesus said, "go into all the world and preach the gospel and care for the hurting." Paul would teach that God put you here to make a difference in His world. Maybe this requirement of Paul is the hardest in the times we live in.

3. The third item needed to know God's will according to Paul is to "be transformed by renewing your mind." - It is hard to know what Paul was referring to in his day. But what about us today? Jesus said we need to choose between two masters: God or Money. That, Jesus said, was the biggest threat to our relationship with Him. I can only assume He would say the same today. God put us here to matter in His world, but the lure of success and money often matter much more. It is usually how we decide our careers, what job we want, and it decides what we are willing to give up to get it. Jesus said, "If you're not willing to give up everything, you can't be My disciple." The philosophy of "if I can afford it, I can have it" seems to be the guide for far too many of those who are Christ-followers. The call from Jesus to "go into all the world with the gospel" takes a back seat to so many things in our lives. Somehow, we need to hear Paul's challenge to renew and to change our focus of what really matters.

Jesus said in Matthew 25, "In as much as you do not care for the hurting in the world, it is the same as not caring about me." Yet, thousands of children, let alone adults, are desperate for help, and even though we know it, we still turn the other way. How do we change that? How do we renew our concern for those Jesus loved so much? How do we change from where our wants outweigh God's wants? Paul says we need to renew, to refresh, and, yes, to change our priorities. We must decide what is important, then we need to begin showing that to our children. Lost people getting found must become a high priority. So, each of us needs to answer Jesus when He asks who is your master, is it money or Me?

Paul's final admonition comes as he says, "Don't think of yourself more highly than you ought to." Be honest about what got you where you are today. If you are wealthy, ask how it happened. Was it me or was it an opportunity God gave to me? Never think that, if you are following Christ, that one career is more important than another. Paul is simply acknowledging that we all need each other. We can all agree that if we all took the same career path, the world would not work. Thank God that some are farmers, some doctors, some engineers, some dentists, some teachers, and some pick up our garbage. We are all part of God's family. Yes, we all need each other. Paul is just reminding us that God has gifted us all differently, so use the gift God gave you to make a difference in God's kingdom.

People's eternal destiny depends on hearing the gospel that must be part of every person's responsibility. Some must go, some must send, some will do both, but we all need to be part of reaching lost people and helping the hurting.

Wouldn't you like to know God's will as you live your life? Wouldn't it be nice to know when you face that tough choice, what does God want you to do? Wouldn't it be nice when your children come and say, "How can

I know God's will," that you could say, yes, I know Romans 12?

If you follow Paul's blueprint here in Romans 12, you will know the answer. But you must be prepared to do all three guidelines. Following just one or two will not do.

Finally, we must accept that all this will not happen at once. This is the process of sanctification that spans our life; it is to become more and more the person God wants us to be.

In 1 Timothy 1-15, Paul wrote: "Here is a trustworthy saying that deserves full acceptance: 'Christ Jesus came into the world to save sinners of whom I am the worst.'" Then in 2 Timothy 4-7, Paul would write, "I have fought the good fight. I have kept the faith." Then Paul concludes in verse 8 by saying, "Now, there is in store for me a crown of righteousness which the Lord, the righteous Judge, will award to me on that day, and not only to me, but also to all who have longed for His appearing.

From the worst of sinners to a crown of righteousness and an eternity with Jesus, that is the testimony of Paul.

I trust that, as you complete this study of Romans, Paul's testimony is yours. It does not matter where you have been, or what you have done, it just matters where you are today.

We said along the way in this study that there are really two choices in your quest for Heaven.

You try hard to live a perfect life knowing you cannot but hope God will grade on a curve, and if you are better than average, He will let you in.

You give up and trust Christ, that His suffering and death was the only payment that can satisfy God's standard of perfection

I hope if you have never trusted Christ alone, this study has convinced you that only the second choice will work. I hope that you will choose today to give up and ask Jesus to forgive you and, in doing so, you will find the same peace that Paul and Martin Luther found. Then you can be as certain of heaven as if you were already there.

CONCLUSION

Where It Began

This study of the book of Romans has forced me once again to look carefully at the message Paul wanted to convey in the chapters we have studied. The overwhelming image I continue to get is of Paul and his passion for the gospel. Paul knew the change it could bring because it happened to him. I grew up in the time of Billy Graham. I have attended his crusades and listened so often to his preaching. What always impressed me was his passion for the gospel that so affected his preaching. It just made you realize this is so important to him. That is Paul and that is the book of Romans that Paul wrote and that book shows his passion. We think of the book of Romans as a theological document, but then, Romans 10 reminds me of the simple gospel message Paul preached: "If you confess with your mouth the Lord Jesus and believe in your heart that God raised Him from the dead, you will be saved." That is the essence of the gospel according to Paul, and that gospel is not complicated but simple. It is the message lost people need to hear to change their eternal destiny.

For Martin Luther, it changed his life and it brought about great change in the church. I wonder if the change that has happened was as much change as Paul or Martin Luther really hoped would happen. The potential change was a mission-minded church, focused on reaching lost people with that simple message that could change their eternal destiny. What we have today is a church divided into hundreds of different denominations, each with a unique teaching on some theological issue they believe is worth separating from the rest. Rather than a mission-focused church, what we have is much more a theology-focused church that is more concerned with being right theologically than reaching lost people. Today, in the same community, we have many different church groups all needing their own building, their own pastor, secretary, office manager, janitor, and, of course, their own building with its debt payments, interest payments, maintenance, utilities, and more.

The mission only comes when all those needs are met. I have been privileged to travel to Africa and India and the pictures of children digging through garbage for something to eat, children with polio because they could not get a vaccine, or children drinking from a stagnant pond of water are images that are hard to forget. It is hard to ignore that so many children are dying before they are five years old because they lack such basic needs the church could provide. I feel the same for the thousands of orphaned children left from wars and HIV aids. This does not deal with the reality that millions of persons around the world have never heard the gospel. We know that thousands more could be reached if funds were available, but rather, we have fancy church buildings to show our priorities. I think of Jesus leaving the temple in Mark 13-1-2. Jesus' disciples want Him to stop and look at the magnificent temple and Jesus seems to say to them, "No, it's not about buildings."

These are the results we have been willing to accept in order to have our own separate groups and our own buildings and, yes, our own version of theology. It seems almost impossible that this is the choice Jesus or Paul, with his passion for the gospel, would ever have accepted. I think of Paul preaching in Athens, saying to the listeners, "The God that I serve does not dwell in temples made with men's hands." Paul knew, as he wrote in Romans 8-9, that God now dwells in the hearts of persons changed by the gospel. I wonder what Paul would have thought if he heard so many pastors welcome people on Sunday morning to "God's House."

When Paul wrote in Romans 7-4, and I paraphrase, "Now that you have died to the law you are free to bear fruit for God," he was pointing to a whole new concept of Christianity that was about fruit-bearing. He seemed to be saying, do good instead of trying to be good. Jesus did that for you. Jesus' final command to his disciples was to go into all the world and change it with the gospel. None of them were theologians, just simple fishermen with a passion to follow Christ. They remembered He had said, "I will make you fishers of men."

Paul, I believe, knew as He wrote this book, the potential it could have on all Christ-followers. I think he knew that the more we knew and understood that our coming to Christ and being adopted into God's family was much more of God's doing than ours. It would change how we lived and how we served. For me it is Paul in Romans 7 painting us a picture of his life before Christ changed him and, then, in Romans 8, showing us what life can be for a Christ-follower. If true, the picture from Romans 8 makes it easy to understand how passionate Paul was and why he wanted to write this letter hoping it would do the same for us.

If this study could help someone understand the "new" and, because of it find the peace that Paul wrote of in Romans 5:1, the same peace that Martin Luther found that changed his life, then this study would have been worthwhile. I grew up in a church where the Heidelberg Catechism was a central part of its theology. The first question is still a central part of what I believe. It asked, "What is your only comfort in life and in death?" The answer—"That I belong body and soul, in life and in death, to my faithful Savior Jesus Christ who has fully paid for all my sin." As I conclude this study of Romans, those words "that I belong" and "fully paid for all my sin" stand out more than before and I truly hope they do for you. We started in Romans chapter 1 suggesting that "living In one's faith" was the real focus of this letter of Romans. My hope is that something in this study has helped make that a reality in your life. Then I know you, too, will know the reality of "Peace with God."

That said, I think of a plaque that hung on the wall of the home I grew up in with the inscription: Only One Life Will Soon Be Past, Only What's Done for Christ Will Last.

I think Paul would have said, "AMEN."

That concludes our study of this amazing letter of Romans.

www.ingramcontent.com/pod-product-compliance
Lightning Source LLC
LaVergne TN
LVHW051101080426
835508LV00019B/2008